CONTENTS

Sex contains all, bodies, souls,
Meanings, proofs, purities, delicacies, results, promulgations,
Songs, commands, health, pride, the maternal mystery, the seminal
    milk
All hopes, benefactions, bestowals, all the passions, loves, beauties,
    delights of the earth,
All the governments, judges, gods, follow'd persons of the earth,
These are contain'd in sex as parts of itself and justifications of
    itself.

Without shame the man I like knows and avows the deliciousness
    of his sex,
Without shame the woman I like knows and avows hers.
                    —Walt Whitman,
                        from "A Woman Waits for Me"

David Lehman was born in New York City in 1948. He is the author of seven books of poems, most recently *When a Woman Loves a Man* (Scribner, 2005). Among his nonfiction books are *The Last Avant-Garde: The Making of the New York School of Poets* (Anchor, 1999) and *The Perfect Murder* (Michigan, 2000). He edited *Great American Prose Poems: From Poe to the Present*, which appeared from Scribner in 2003. He teaches writing and literature in the graduate writing program of the New School in New York City and offers an undergraduate course each fall on "Great Poems" at NYU. He edited the new edition of *The Oxford Book of American Poetry*, a one-volume comprehensive anthology of poems from Anne Bradstreet to the present. Lehman has collaborated with James Cummins on a book of sestinas, *Jim and Dave Defeat the Masked Man* (Soft Skull), and with Judith Hall on a "pl'em," or "play poem," combining words and images, *Poetry Forum* (Bayeux Arts). He initiated the *Best American Poetry* series in 1988 and received a Guggenheim Fellowship a year later. He lives in New York City and in Ithaca, New York.

INTRODUCTION

by David Lehman

In *My Secret Life* (c. 1890), that classic work of late-Victorian pornography, the author, an anonymous gentleman with a raging libido and the compulsion to repeat and record his amatory adventures, writes, "Providence has made the continuation of the species depend on a process of coupling the sexes, called fucking. . . . It is not a graceful operation—in fact it is not more elegant than pissing, or shitting, and is more ridiculous; but it is one giving the intensest pleasure to the parties operating together, and most people try to do as much of it as they can." The artless simplicity of these sentences is their charm, though they are more complicated than meets the eye. Notice the relation of "coupling" to the perpetuation of the species on the one hand and to superlative pleasure on the other. The conjugation of the bodies is the observance of a sacrament, a religious imperative, but it also involves the unrelentingly gross human body in an "operation" no finer than urination or defecation, and "more ridiculous."

Call it fucking or call it making love: The "process of coupling" is the fact at the center of all erotic speculation. *Fucking* remains the ultimate profanity. The word's effect is like that of the tarot card of the lovers dealt upside down: the same meaning in the form of its negative inversion. But any word or phrase for sexual intercourse, euphemistic and genteel, or clinical and precise, or lewd and graphic, will prove inadequate to the ramifications of the act. The many possible ways of talking about *it,* that great pronoun—or as Freud would have it, *id*— suggest that contradictory impulses are at work, or contradictory ways of presenting the same impulse. An instance of heterosexual love, for example, can be depicted as the union of yin and yang, husband and wife engaged in the blessed task of procreation, or contrarily, as an anomalous episode during a temporary truce in the battle between the sexes. In any case, we know that sexual desire is a drive that seems to trump all others and dictate human behavior, sometimes against all reason or beyond any rational explanation. We know that it is the most intense and irresistible of bawdy pleasures, that it makes fools and rascals and buffoons of us and often lowers the attitudinal level from tragic postures and epic vistas to bedroom farces and comedies of Eros. Yet as Anonymous noted in 1890, "most people try to do as much of it as they can," and everyone thinks about it more than anyone will admit.

Classical images of Eros—or Cupid, as the Romans renamed him—show an infant archer or, in Jacques-Louis David's famous painting, an impishly grinning young man with angel wings beside his sleeping beauty, Psyche, embodiment of the eternal feminine. It is not difficult to decode the symbolism. That Cupid is depicted as a baby points to the inevitable consequences of sex, and you are left to wonder whether the child to come is a penalty for a guilty pleasure, an extra mouth to feed, or a reward. According to Apuleius in *The Golden Ass,* Psyche can link with her lover Cupid only at night and on condition that she not see his face. Given that Psyche means *mind* or *soul* in Greek, can the myth be a parable in disguise? Not that use of a blindfold may produce excellent results, but that the soul's yearning for erotic fulfillment can and does happen, albeit with strings attached that are easy to break, as Psyche learns to her consternation in Apuleius.

The familiar image of the "beast with two backs" is ridiculous but accurate and therefore a valuable corrective to high-minded or romantic representations of the theme. A more flattering image comes from George Bernard Shaw. Dancing, in Shaw's words, is "a perpendicular expression of a horizontal desire." (This is just one reason to lament the passing of an era when ballroom dancing was universal.) The subject of sex gives rise to elegant aphorism ("Sex is the lyricism of the masses," Charles Baudelaire), extravagantly mixed metaphor ("Sex is a black tarantula and sex without religion is like an egg without salt," Luis Buñuel), and exceedingly clever limerick ("An Argentine gaucho named Bruno / Declared there is one thing I do know: / A woman is fine, / A boy is divine, / But a llama is numero uno"). Sex in *The Waste Land* is a nightmare from which the typist may never recover, consisting of passionless caresses, "unreproved, if undesired," from "the young man carbuncular"—surely the least desirable epithet ever conferred on a man. But then T. S. Eliot's poem is an example of what Lee Upton calls "dyserotica," which bears the same relation to the erotic as the worldview of *1984* or *Brave New World* does to *Utopia*.

Sex entered literature from the first. Look at Homer. The event propelling *The Iliad* is a conflict between two warriors over the sexual favors of a concubine, as if the abduction of Helen by Paris—the cause of the entire Trojan War—was pretty much standard practice for that time and place. The hero of *The Odyssey,* the apotheosis of the

Greek masculine ideal, is so magnificent a specimen that goddesses, demigoddesses, and daughters of kings love him, wish to possess him, and do not want to let him go. You can blame Poseidon, god of the sea, for the twenty years it takes Odysseus to reach Ithaka and reclaim his Penelope. But I think the wiles and designs of Calypso and Circe had something to do with it as well.

English lyric poetry (excluded from this anthology for practical considerations but not for lack of love) got its start with the conventions of courtly love, one prime manifestation of Eros. The greatly undervalued Fulke Greville writes with zest of his darling Cynthia, "naked on a bed of play." The seventeenth-century Cavalier poet Robert Herrick has a phrase as sexy as any I have heard about the effect of clothes on the body of the beloved: "When as in silks my Julia goes, / Then, then (me thinks) how sweetly flowes / That liquefaction of her clothes." From plainspoken Philip Larkin (1922–1985), who fancied himself "less deceived" than most, we get a rueful little history lesson: "Sexual intercourse began / In nineteen sixty-three / (Which was rather late for me)— / Between the end of the *Chatterley* ban / And the Beatles' first LP." From the Earl of Rochester's sharp pen comes a rake's raunchy oath: "O that I now could, by some chemic art, / To sperm convert my vitals and my heart, / That at one thrust I might my soul translate, / And in the womb myself regenerate: / There steep'd in lust, nine months I would remain; / Then boldly fuck my passage out again."

In the English canon, I have a special affection for the seduction poems of John Donne and Andrew Marvell. Donne issued robust commands and adorned them in the most outlandish of poetic conceits. The female body becomes the map of the world: "License my roving hands, and let them go / Before, behind, between, above, below. / O my America! my new-found-land." Marvell's "To His Coy Mistress" is a monument to Latin logic (we're young, time's flying, act now) and features the sort of naughty pun that has delighted generations of English majors. Having praised his lady hyperbolically in the poem's first stanza, Marvell heartlessly threatens her in the next with an image of untimely death: "then worms shall try / That long-preserved virginity, / And your quaint honor turn to dust, / And into ashes all my lust." The pun on *quaint*—from the medieval *queinte,* the word from which *cunt* derives—enhances a poem that epitomizes seventeenth-century metaphysical wit. You're meant to hear an echo of "The Miller's Tale," the bawdiest of Chaucer's *Canterbury*

Tales, in which a cunning clerk catches a lithesome lass "by the *queinte.*" Chaucer is writing a ribald and bawdy narrative, Marvell a seduction poem with a carpe diem argument. The two works couldn't differ more dramatically. Yet I would not hesitate to characterize each as erotic—as is, for that matter, the Song of Songs in the Old Testament: "Thou hast ravished my heart, my sister, my spouse; thou hast ravished my heart with one of thine eyes, with one bead of thy necklace. How fair is thy love, my sister, my spouse! how much better is thy love than wine! And the smell of thine ointments than all spices!"

In the realm of the erotic, the sacred and the profane converge, and so do the sublime and the ridiculous. The overlapping of sexual and religious impulses in art and literature is too marked to go unnoticed. Take, for example, Donne's "holy sonnet" beginning "Batter my heart, three-personed God." The poet presents his relation to God as that of a submissive lover begging to be overmastered. He concludes with rapid-fire paradoxes and pleas: "Take me to You, imprison me, for I, / Except You enthrall me, never shall be free, / Nor ever chaste, except You ravish me." In some of Emily Dickinson's poems, as in the Donne sonnet, the sexual imagery serves a religious intent, yet the reader suspects that if you flip the terms *sexual* and *religious* in that clause, it would work equally well. The erotically obsessed Graham Greene, a sincere Catholic and unreformed adulterer, has a remarkable novel, *The End of the Affair,* in which the hero loses his lover not to her husband but to a much more formidable adversary—the divinity whom she worships devoutly in church. It's as if to say that Augustine (as he implies in his *Confessions*) could as easily have been a sinner as a saint, and with equal passion. For sex is as ancient a ritual, as formidable an imperative, and as elemental an instinct as the impulses to worship and to pray.

Nin Andrews remembers the first time she heard of Eros. Nin was in first grade, and her mother would read aloud to her at night, alternating Bible stories and Greek myths. "One night Mom read of Hades kidnapping Persephone," she recalls. "Another night King David saw Bathsheba bathing. 'Why are these men so bad?' I asked. My mother's answer: 'It's when they're bad that the story is good, isn't it?'" Yes, bad behavior is almost always more erotic than good. "Christianity," according to the French novelist Anatole France, "has done a great deal for love by making a sin out of it." The transgressive nature of much sexual behavior acts more often as an inducement than as a deterrent, and though some very good poems about lawful wedded bliss do get written, an atmosphere of sinfulness and secrecy, of clandestine assignations and furtive infidelities, permeates much of the best erotic writing. In Greene's novels, for example, espionage is either an excuse for sexual adventure or a metaphor for it, danger fused with thrill. The id is a rebel angel. Though God instructs Adam to "be fruitful and multiply"—it is the first commandment in Genesis—the sexual means to this end are associated with disobedience. The act of linking their bodies is what Adam and Eve do to consummate their original sin of eating from the tree of knowledge, and *carnal knowledge* is a beautiful euphemism for copulation considered as a way of passing forbidden knowledge between bodies. And after Adam and Eve have sex and sleep it off, they wake to the consciousness of guilt and the end of public nudity.

The nature of desire, that force or drive that overpowers the will, blinds the eyes, and clouds the rational mind, is a subject in many poems of Eros. Strict constructionists of the erotic argue for the centrality of longing and desire. They feel instinctively that for a poem to qualify as erotic, it has to lead to arousal or quicken desire. I favor a more elastic definition. There is room here for love and wanton lust; for the imp of the perverse, all forms of ardor, all manner of fetish; for rhapsodies of wild nights and rapturous dawns. But I grant the larger point: The heart of the erotic lies not in fulfillment but in desire. As Barbara Lazear Ascher puts it in her book *Dancing in the Dark* (1999), the erotic heat is "in the longing not the humping." *Desire*: It is a peculiarity of the word that it rhymes with *fire* (as in Robert Frost's end-of-the-world poem "Fire and Ice") and with a synonym for need. Let William Blake demonstrate in his four-line poem "The Question Answered": "What is it men in women do require? / The lineaments of Gratified Desire. / What is it women in men do require? / The lineaments of Gratified Desire."

The idea for this book springs from twin observations about American poetry. Even before launching an annual anthology monitoring the contemporary scene, I couldn't help noticing that poets, especially younger poets, and younger women above all, were writing with unusual candor and passion and often with intelligence and wit about their sexual relationships. It was all fair game, the whole erotic circle leading from initial attraction to bittersweet after-the-fact rumination and back, with plenty of stops along the way for insults, quarrels, kisses, morals, seduction, foreplay, coition, orgasm, and postcoital tristesse. The tendency has grown even bolder in the last twenty years. Poets are examining the erotic life from all angles and every point of view. They are writing poems based on autobiographical episodes and flamboyant fantasies, poems about body parts and about the very vocabulary we use for our sexual organs, and they are using all the devices at their disposal. They are writing sonnets and sestinas, pantoums and prose poems, ballads and blues. In these pages you will encounter all of the above plus a villanelle, an epigram, an ode to semen, more than one meditation on masturbation, an aubade to greet the dawn and a "late" aubade to justify staying in bed, letters from lover to lover, a dream of universal nudity, and a dream song to infiltrate the sleeping mind in much the way that Cupid joined Pysche in the deepest dark of the night.

The second observation from which this book springs is the recognition that there exists a vital American tradition of erotic poetry. I am thinking of Walt Whitman celebrating the human body and Emily Dickinson contemplating the nectars of Eden, of Edgar Allan Poe's obsession with another man's bride and Edith Wharton's postscript to a night of abandon, of Emma Lazarus's dream of a secret kiss and Gertrude Stein's hymn to "lifting belly." As I read for this book, works of superb sensuality surfaced from sources expected (E. E. Cummings) and unlikely if known at all (Isabella Stewart Gardner). A poem by Francis Scott Key in appreciation of a nubile young woman espied in the nudity of her "shower bath" came as a big surprise. Nor had I previously encountered the suite of short poems written by the aging Kenneth Rexroth in the voice of a young Japanese woman. Among my favorite works in *The Best American Erotic Poems* is one that Hart Crane wrote at the age of twenty about a man bandaging the hand of a man injured in a factory accident. The subject of "Episode of Hands" is medical. But in its language and imagery, it is extraordinarily erotic: "The gash was bleeding, and a shaft of sun / That glittered in and out among the wheels, / Fell lightly, warmly, down into the wound." I agree with Ron Horning's assessment: " 'Episode of Hands' is as close to Cavafy as any American has ever gotten."

W. H. Auden's "The Platonic Blow" is a camp classic, an over-the-top ballad portraying the ideal blowjob. Auden wrote it in New York in 1948 and relished its composition, but he later disavowed it and never claimed copyright. With its flourishes of rhyme and rhetoric, the poem survived for a long time on its underground circulation.

But the impulse to censor or self-censor is much less strong today than when Auden began his poem with the smell of the locker room on a spring day, making it "a day for a lay" or "a day to blow or get blown." I didn't think twice about including "The Platonic Blow," which is so well crafted that it blurs any line you can draw between erotica and pornography. The case against Robert Frost's "The Subverted Flower" is that the scenario described therein will not quicken your libido or warm your heart. But I contend that sexual failure, as common as it is unfortunate, has its place in the literature of Eros. And this dark and uncanny poem begs to be read, interpreted, and discussed in the context of the erotic.

Readers of pornography on the judicial bench claim that they can't define it but know it when they see it. That is as good an approach as any and has the virtue of implying that all the verbiage on the subject has left us little wiser. You can safely say that pornography "appeals to the prurient interest," whereas erotica has "literary or artistic value." The key word in that formulation is "value," and certainly, in the making of this book, I wanted poems that have added value to our lives and our culture. As I always do when working on an anthology, I welcomed suggestions from friends, colleagues, and students, and what amazed me was how little agreement there was. The disputes were less about the literary quality of the work in review than about whether it was sufficiently erotic. One person recommended Robert Lowell's "Man and Wife," in which the married couple has taken tranquilizers, the woman is asleep with her back to the man, and there is a heavy sadness in the air that I took as the very antithesis of the erotic. I know that readers will approach the contents of this book with its title in mind and that therefore poems of a certain subtlety or covert sexual agenda will fit nicely. But I also know that no definition will come in handy to justify my decision to include Frost's "Subverted Flower" and not Lowell's "Man and Wife." It is finally a matter of judgment, instinct, and nerve, and the editor has no choice but to trust his own responses to the serious contenders. Every poem in this book has given me pleasure, most of them have taught me something, and the general assembly delights me with its variety and energy.

Following William Gass in *On Being Blue* (1976), I believe there are multiple ways that sex can enter a work of writing, including "direct depiction," the use of "sexual words," "displacement" (the use of metaphor), and "the use of language like a lover." I wanted examples of all these. Gass's idea that the act of writing can itself be erotic makes a lot of sense to me. There are poems that display, in his words, "not the language of love, but the love of language, not matter, but meaning, not what the tongue touches, but what it forms, not lips and nipples, but nouns and verbs." I am partial to wit in poetry and was intent on including comic and satiric poems in a variety of registers, but I was also deeply attracted to poems that had the sort of hot-blooded passion that you find superbly in D. H. Lawrence. "Be still when you have nothing to say," Lawrence wrote. "When genuine passion moves you, say what you've got to say, and say it hot."

Over a hundred years after Freud and his disciples argued for the centrality of sex in the formation of the human personality, what was once a contention has become an axiom. Hormones reign and sex sells. If anything, the amount of sex in our cultural life has grown. Nudity onstage in theatrical productions of *Marat/Sade* and *Oh! Calcutta!* was sensational in the 1960s but is no big deal today. We are, says the *New Republic* columnist Britt Peterson, "awash in raunch culture." She tells of "alt-porn, a new hipster genre" of movie, in which "the smut itself is becoming more upper-middle-class: urbane, ironic, self-aware, and intellectually as well as sexually titillating."[1] Eve Fairbanks, another *New Republic* diarist, is okay with the knowledge that if you Google her name, you get links to "rambling, bawdy paragraphs done in a stream-of-consciousness, misspelled, arbitrarily capitalized style, like a dirty parody of *Finnegans Wake*." The Internet has lifted veils, opened closets, and made a host of fetishes and perversities seem not exactly normal or routine but ubiquitous and therefore legitimate. If every individual can aspire to his or her own website, the value has to be on disclosure, not reticence. "Teens blog details, true or made up, about their personal lives that their elders would have blushed to put in their diaries."[2] Women's erotica has taken off as a publishing category somewhere between mass romance and outright porn. Sample titles: *Bound, Big Guns out of Uniform,* and *Gotta Have It.*[3] In *The Atlantic,* Caitlin Flanagan reports on the "teenage oral-sex craze" and wonders how it

1. Britt Peterson, "Porn with a Silver Spoon" (*The New Republic,* June 4, 2007), p. 64.
2. Eve Fairbanks, "The Porn Identity" (*The New Republic,* February 6, 2006), p. 34.
3. Matthew Flam, "More Heat Between the Covers" (*Crain's New York Business,* February 20, 2006), p. 37.

came about that America's girls are "on their knees." All over Chicago, where Flanagan lives, "in the very best schools, in the nicest families, in the leafiest neighborhoods, twelve- and thirteen-year-old girls are performing oral sex on as many boys as they can."[4] Flanagan is appalled at the phenomenon. Christopher Hitchens in *Vanity Fair* is breezy in contrast as he propounds the view that the blowjob is America's "signature sex act." Hitchens talks about *Deep Throat, Portnoy's Complaint, Lolita,* and *The Godfather,* not to mention the fabled Oval Office vestibule in the Clinton White House, in pursuit of his story: "how America grabbed the Olympic scepter of the blowjob and held on tight."[5]

In this context it is not a surprise that poets would write openly and rhapsodically about their sexual lives and dreams. What is eye-opening are the lusty freedom and literary skill with which they have celebrated their erotic imaginations. When I am asked to talk about new trends, the emergence of a voluptuous body of erotic poems is almost always first on my list. It seems that nothing is off-limits to the contemporary poet. Office sex, first sex, oral sex, cyber-sex ("in a tangle of Internet"), solo sex, sex from the other's point of view, voyeurism, bondage, parables of gardens with snakes, allegories of flowers and bees, dreams of horses or swans, and the use of a gin bottle as a surrogate lover: They're all here. And no terms are forbidden from use. There is almost a mini-genre of poems devoted to the attractions and drawbacks of such words as *fuck, cunt, pussy,* and *orgasm.* Not that the liberal sprinkling of profanities assures anyone of anything. "I cannot honestly say I see any noteworthy improvement in our life, thought, or writing, now that 'fuck' can be heard and seen in public," William Gass wrote in *On Being Blue,* "because its appearance is as unmeant and hypocritical as its former absence was. We fear to seem a prude." Point well taken: Marlon Brando in an undershirt clinching with Eva Marie Saint in a slip (in *On the Water-front,* 1954), or Rita Hayworth and Orson Welles embracing on a yacht (in *The Lady from Shanghai,* 1948), will get your blood going faster than any number of nude scenes in more recent films. Nevertheless, the greater freedom of vocabulary in tandem with a loosening of

4. Caitlin Flanagan, "Are You There God? It's Me, Monica" (*The Atlantic Monthly,* January/February 2006), p. 167.
5. Christopher Hitchens, "As American as Apple Pie" (*Vanity Fair,* July 2006), p. 54.

moral or religious restraint has spurred poets to tackle subjects formerly taboo, and they have done so with such freshness and style that you can't help taking notice. For the sake of inclusiveness and variety, I decided to limit each poet (except Emily Dickinson) to one poem. For reasons of space, the unkindest cuts of all had to be made at the last minute. I had to shelve so many worthy poems that I could have made a second anthology approximately the length of this one. The dates given in parentheses following the poems refer usually to year of publication, easier to ascertain than year of composition. In lieu of the conventional biographical note, I have asked the contributors to write a paragraph about their all-time favorite work of erotic writing, any genre, any language, any period. The preferences registered thus far include the Song of Songs, *The Tale of Genji, The Story of O,* Shakespeare, "No Platonic Love" by the seventeenth-century poet William Cartwright, Robert Herrick, John Donne, Andrew Marvell, Rainer Maria Rilke, Pablo Neruda, E. E. Cummings, Vladimir Nabokov, Anaïs Nin, Marguerite Duras, Frank O'Hara, and Edward Gorey. Seven of the poems in this volume have been named as contributors' personal favorites: W. H. Auden's "The Platonic Blow," Emily Dickinson's "Come slowly—Eden!" and "Wild Nights—Wild Nights!," Galway Kinnell's "Last Gods," Adrienne Rich's "(The Floating Poem, Unnumbered)," Charles Simic's "Breasts," and Gertrude Stein's *Lifting Belly.* Other contributors (such as Walt Whitman, E. E. Cummings, Dennis Cooper, Jennifer L. Knox, Paul Muldoon, John Updike, and Sharon Olds) are also cited as exemplars. The range of opinion is wide, and it's my hope that people will consult these notes as one would consult an annotated reading list on this most irresistible of subjects.

Although there is plenty of competition, I would cast my own vote for the modern Greek poet C. P. Cavafy (1863–1933). I have long loved such of his poems as "Days of 1908" (trans. James Merrill), "The Next Table" and "Body, Remember . . ." (trans. Edmund Keeley and Philip Sherrard), and "The Tobacco Shop Window" and "Their Origin" (trans. Theoharis C. Theoharis). Gore Vidal calls Cavafy "the Pindar of the one-night stand between males." I admire the frank sensuality of Cavafy's poems, the way he balances memory and desire. He can capture remembered lovers and affairs without falling into the usual traps; he doesn't overwrite or sentimentalize his feelings. He is a truth-teller. There is a little poem entitled "One Night" in which Cavafy quite characteristically contrasts the gorgeous fever of lovemaking with the humble or seedy circumstances in which it takes place. Emboldened by Nin Andrews, who composed her note on César Vallejo in verse, I have done the same in crafting this imitation of "One Night":

POEM IN THE MANNER OF C. P. CAVAFY

The room had a bed with torn sheets
above the bar where I met her
on Tuesdays in June and July.
And the light was bad, and there were
holes in the screens in the windows
where flies and mosquitoes
came in with the heat
and the laughter of the workers
playing poker downstairs.

And in that narrow room stinking
of cigarette smoke I breathed in
the bliss that only the young
and invincible know when
her young breasts rose and pressed
against my chest, and I was drunk
on her kisses and all these years later
I am drunk again though alone
as I think of those nights with her.

Ithaca, NY
July 2007

THE BEST AMERICAN
EROTIC POEMS

∾

On a Young Lady's Going into a Shower Bath

"O that this too too solid flesh would melt
Thaw and resolve itself" to water clear,
And pure as that which flows through flowery vales
Of Arcady, and stays its gentle wave
To kiss the budding blossoms on its brink,
Or to encircle in its fond embrace
Some trembling, blushing maid, who doubting stands,
And hopes and fears to trust the smiling stream!
Then, as the amorous rise of Gods and men
From Heav'n descended in a golden show'r
To Danaë's open arms, another heav'n
So from the bath, that o'er the shrinking charms
Of Sweet Nerea hung, would I more blest
Than rapturous love, upon a form more fair
Than Danaë's a silver show'r descends.
O then those charms of which the lighted touch
Would fire the frozen blood of apathy,
Each drop of me should touch, should eager run
Down her fair forehead, down her blushing cheek
To taste the more inviting sweets beneath,
Should trickle down her neck, should slowly wind,
In silver circles round those hills of snow,
Or lingering steal through the sweet vale between
And when at length perplex'd with the rich store
Of nature's varied, most luxuriant charms,
Amid the circling tendrils which entwine
An altar form'd for love's soft sacrifice,
Insinuating creep, there as a bee
In a fresh rosebud hid, a refuge find
From the rude napkin's sacrilegious touch.

(1857)

Song

I saw thee on thy bridal day—
  When a burning blush came o'er thee,
Though happiness around thee lay,
  The world all love before thee:

And in thine eye a kindling light
  (Whatever it might be)
Was all on Earth my aching sight
  Of Loveliness could see.

That blush, perhaps, was maiden shame—
  As such it well may pass—
Though its glow hath raised a fiercer flame
  In the breast of him, alas!

Who saw thee on that bridal day,
  When that deep blush *would* come o'er thee,
Though happiness around thee lay,
  The world all love before thee.

(1827)

I Sing the Body Electric

1

The bodies of men and women engirth me, and I engirth them,
They will not let me off nor I them till I go with them and respond
  to them and love them.

Was it doubted if those who corrupt their own live bodies conceal
  themselves?
And if those who defile the living are as bad as they who defile the
  dead?

2

The expression of the body of man or woman balks account,
The male is perfect and that of the female is perfect.

The expression of a well-made man appears not only in his face,
It is in his limbs and joints also, it is curiously in the joints of his
  hips and wrists,
It is in his walk, the carriage of his neck, the flex of his waist and
  knees—dress does not hide him,
The strong sweet supple quality he has strikes through the cotton and
  flannel,
To see him pass conveys as much as the best poem, perhaps more,
You linger to see his back and the back of his neck and shoulder-side.

The sprawl and fulness of babes, the bosoms and heads of women,
  the folds of their dress, their style as we pass in the street, the
  contour of their shape downwards,
The swimmer naked in the swimming-bath, seen as he swims through
  the salt transparent green-shine, or lies on his back and rolls silently
  with the heave of the water,

Framers bare-armed framing a house, hoisting the beams in their places,
    or using the mallet and mortising-chisel,
The bending forward and backward of rowers in row-boats—the
    horseman in his saddle,
Girls and mothers and housekeepers in all their exquisite offices,
The group of laborers seated at noon-time with their open dinner-kettles,
    and their wives waiting,
The female soothing a child—the farmer's daughter in the garden or
    cow-yard,
The young fellow hoeing corn—the sleigh-driver guiding his six horses
    through the crowd,
The wrestle of wrestlers, two apprentice-boys, quite grown, lusty,
    good-natured, native-born, out on the vacant lot at sun-down
    after work,
The coats vests and caps thrown down, the embrace of love and
    resistance,
The upper-hold and under-hold—the hair rumpled over and blinding
    the eyes,
The march of firemen in their own costumes—the play of the masculine
    muscle through clean-setting trowsers and waist-straps,
The slow return from the fire, the pause when the bell strikes
    suddenly again—the listening on the alert,
The natural perfect and varied attitudes—the bent head, the curved
    neck, the counting:
Such-like I love—I loosen myself and pass freely—and am at the
    mother's breast with the little child,
And swim with the swimmer, and wrestle with the wrestlers, and
    march in line with the firemen, and pause and listen and count.

3

I knew a man—he was a common farmer—he was the father of
    five sons—and in them were the fathers of sons—and in them
    were the fathers of sons.

This man was a wonderful vigor and calmness and beauty of person,
The shape of his head, the richness and breadth of his manners, the
    pale yellow and white of his hair and beard, the immeasurable
    meaning of his black eyes,
These I used to go and visit him to see—he was wise also,

He was six feet tall—he was over eighty years old—his sons were
 massive clean bearded tan-faced and handsome,
They and his daughters loved him—all who saw him loved him—
 they did not love him by allowance—they loved him with
 personal love,
He drank water only—the blood showed like scarlet through the
 clear-brown skin of his face,
He was a frequent gunner and fisher—he sailed his boat himself—he
 had a fine one presented to him by a ship-joiner—he had fowling-
 pieces, presented to him by men that loved him,
When he went with his five sons and many grand-sons to hunt or fish
 you would pick him out as the most beautiful and vigorous of
 the gang,
You would wish long and long to be with him—you would wish to
 sit by him in the boat that you and he might touch each other.

4

I have perceived that to be with those I like is enough,
To stop in company with the rest at evening is enough,
To be surrounded by beautiful curious breathing laughing flesh is
 enough,
To pass among them, to touch any one, to rest my arm ever so lightly
 round his or her neck for a moment—what is this then?

I do not ask any more delight—I swim in it as in a sea.

There is something in staying close to men and women and looking
 on them and in the contact and odor of them that pleases the
 soul well,
All things please the soul, but these please the soul well.

5

This is the female form,
A divine nimbus exhales from it from head to foot,
It attracts with fierce undeniable attraction,
I am drawn by its breath as if I were no more than a helpless vapor—
 all falls aside but myself and it,

Books, art, religion, time, the visible and solid earth, the atmosphere
and the fringed clouds, what was expected of heaven or feared
of hell are now consumed,
Mad filaments, ungovernable shoots play out of it, the response
likewise ungovernable,
Hair, bosom, hips, bend of legs, negligent falling hands—all diffused—
mine too diffused,
Ebb stung by the flow, and flow stung by the ebb—love-flesh swelling
and deliciously aching,
Limitless limpid jets of love hot and enormous, quivering jelly of love,
white-blow and delirious juice,
Bridegroom night of love working surely and softly into the prostrate
dawn,
Undulating into the willing and yielding day,
Lost in the cleave of the clasping and sweet-fleshed day.

This is the nucleus—after the child is born of woman the man is born
of woman,
This is the bath of birth—this is the merge of small and large and the
outlet again.

Be not ashamed women—your privilege encloses the rest, it is the exit
of the rest,
You are the gates of the body and you are the gates of the soul.

The female contains all qualities and tempers them—she is in her
place—she moves with perfect balance,
She is all things duly veiled—she is both passive and active—she is to
conceive daughters as well as sons and sons as well as daughters.

As I see my soul reflected in nature, as I see through a mist one with
inexpressible completeness and beauty, see the bent head and
arms folded over the breast—the female I see.

6

The male is not less the soul, nor more—he too is in his place,
He too is all qualities—he is action and power—the flush of the
known universe is in him,

Scorn becomes him well and appetite and defiance become him well,
The fiercest largest passions, a bliss that is utmost and sorrow that is
    utmost become him well—pride is for him,
The full-spread pride of man is calming and excellent to the soul,
Knowledge becomes him—he likes it always—he brings everything
    to the test of himself,
Whatever the survey, whatever the sea and the sail, he strikes
    soundings at last only here,
Where else does he strike soundings except here?

The man's body is sacred and the woman's body is sacred, it is no
    matter who,
Is it a slave? Is it one of the dull-faced immigrants just landed on the
    wharf?

Each belongs here or anywhere just as much as the well-off—just as
    much as you,
Each has his or her place in the procession.

All is a procession,
The universe is a procession with measured and perfect motion.
Do you know so much yourself that you call the slave or the dull-face
    ignorant?
Do you suppose you have a right to a good sight, and he or she has
    no right to a sight?
Do you think matter has cohered together from its diffused float, and
    the soil is on the surface and water runs and vegetation sprouts
    for you only, and not for him and her?

7

A slave at auction!
I help the auctioneer—the sloven does not half know his business.

Gentlemen look on this curious creature,
Whatever the bids of the bidders they cannot be high enough for him,
For him the globe lay preparing quintillions of years without one
    animal or plant,
For him the revolving cycles truly and steadily rolled.

7

In this head the all-baffling brain,
In it and below it the making of the attributes of heroes.

Examine these limbs, red black or white—they are very cunning in
    tendon and nerve,
They shall be stript that you may see them.

Exquisite senses, life-lit eyes, pluck, volition,
Flakes of breast-muscle, pliant backbone and neck, flesh not flabby,
    good-sized arms and legs,
And wonders within there yet.

Within there runs his blood, the same old blood, the same red
    running blood,
There swells and jets his heart—there all passions and desires—all
    reachings and aspirations,
Do you think they are not there because they are not expressed in
    parlors and lecture-rooms?

This is not only one man, he is the father of those who shall be fathers
    in their turns,
In him the start of populous states and rich republics,
Of him countless immortal lives with countless embodiments and
    enjoyments.

How do you know who shall come from the offspring of his offspring
    through the centuries?
Who might you find you have come from yourself if you could trace
    back through the centuries?

8

A woman at auction,
She too is not only herself—she is the teeming mother of mothers,
She is the bearer of them that shall grow and be mates to the mothers.

Her daughters or their daughters' daughters—who knows who shall
    mate with them?
Who knows through the centuries what heroes may come from them?

In them and of them natal love—in them the divine mystery—the same
old beautiful mystery.

Have you ever loved a woman?
Your mother—is she living? have you been much with her? and has
she been much with you?
Do you not see that these are exactly the same to all in all nations and
times all over the earth?
If life and the soul are sacred the human body is sacred,
And the glory and sweet of a man is the token of manhood untainted,
And in man or woman a clean strong firm-fibred body is beautiful as
the most beautiful face.

Have you seen the fool that corrupted his own live body? or the fool
that corrupted her own live body?
For they do not conceal themselves, and cannot conceal themselves.

Who degrades or defiles the living human body is cursed,
Who degrades or defiles the body of the dead is not more cursed.

9

O my body! I dare not desert the likes of you in other men and
women, nor the likes of the parts of you;
I believe the likes of you are to stand or fall with the likes of the soul,
(and that they are the soul,)
I believe the likes of you shall stand or fall with my poems—and that
they are poems,
Man's, woman's, child's, youth's, wife's, husband's, mother's,
father's, young man's, young woman's poems,
Head, neck, hair, ears, drop and tympan of the ears,
Eyes, eye-fringes, iris of the eye, eye-brows, and the waking or
sleeping of the lids,
Mouth, tongue, lips, teeth, roof of the mouth, jaws, and
the jaw-hinges,
Nose, nostrils of the nose, and the partition,
Cheeks, temples, forehead, chin, throat, back of the neck, neck-slue,
Strong shoulders, manly beard, scapula, hind-shoulders, and the
ample side-round of the chest,

Upper-arm, arm-pit, elbow-socket, lower-arm, arm-sinews,
    arm-bones,
Wrist and wrist-joints, hand, palm, knuckles, thumb, fore-finger,
    finger-balls, finger-joints, finger-nails,
Broad breast-front, curling hair of the breast, breast-bone, breast-side,
Ribs, belly, back-bone, joints of the back-bone,
Hips, hip-sockets, hip-strength, inward and outward round,
    man-balls, man-root,
Strong set of thighs, well carrying the trunk above,
Leg-fibres, knee, knee-pan, upper-leg, under-leg,
Ankles, instep, foot-ball, toes, toe-joints, the heel,
All attitudes, all the shapeliness, all the belongings of my or your body,
    or of any one's body, male or female,
The lung-sponges, the stomach-sac, the bowels sweet and clean,
The brain in its folds inside the skull-frame,
Sympathies, heart-valves, palate-valves, sexuality, maternity,
Womanhood, and all that is a woman—and the man that comes from
    woman,
The womb, the teats, nipples, breast-milk, tears, laughter, weeping,
    love-looks, love-perturbations and risings,
The voice, articulation, language, whispering, shouting aloud,
Food, drink, pulse, digestion, sweat, sleep, walking, swimming,
Poise on the hips, leaping, reclining, embracing, arm-curving, and
    tightening,
The continual changes of the flex of the mouth, and around the eyes,
The skin, the sun-burnt shade, freckles, hair,
The curious sympathy one feels, when feeling with the hand the
    naked meat of his own body, or another person's body,
The circling rivers, the breath, and breathing it in and out,
The beauty of the waist, and thence of the hips, and thence downward
    toward the knees,
The thin red jellies within you, or within me—the bones, and the
    marrow in the bones,
The exquisite realization of health,
O I think now these are not the parts and poems of the body only,
    but of the soul,
O I think these are the soul!

(1855–1856)

GEORGE HENRY BOKER (1823–1890)

from *Sonnets: A Sequence on Profane Love*

If she should give me all I ask of her,
The virgin treasures of her modest love;
If lip to lip in eager frenzy clove,
And limb with limb should palpitate and stir
In that wild struggle whose delights confer
A rapture which the jealous gods above
Envy and long for as they coldly move
Through votive fumes of spice and burning myrrh;
Yea, were her beauty thus securely mine,
Forever waiting at my beck and call,
I lord and master of her all in all;
Yet at that weakness I would fret and pine
Which makes exhausted nature trip and fall
Just at the point where it becomes divine.

(1929)

EMILY DICKINSON (1830–1886)

∾

211

Come slowly—Eden!
Lips unused to Thee—
Bashful—sip thy Jessamines—
As the fainting Bee—

Reaching late his flower,
Round her chamber hums—
Counts his nectars—
Enters—and is lost in Balms.

(c. 1860)

249

Wild Nights—Wild Nights!
Were I with thee
Wild Nights should be
Our luxury!

Futile—the Winds—
To a Heart in port—
Done with the Compass—
Done with the Chart!

Rowing in Eden—
Ah, the Sea!
Might I but moor—Tonight—
In Thee!

(1861)

315

He fumbles at your Soul
As Players at the Keys
Before they drop full Music on—
He stuns you by degrees—
Prepares your brittle Nature
For the Ethereal Blow
By fainter Hammers—further heard—
Then nearer—Then so slow
Your Breath has time to straighten—
Your Brain—to bubble Cool—
Deals—One—imperial—Thunderbolt—
That scalps your naked Soul—

When Winds take Forests in the Paws—
The Universe—is still—

(1862)

1555

I groped for him before I knew
With solemn nameless need
All other bounty sudden chaff
For this foreshadowed Food
Which others taste and spurn and sneer—
Though I within suppose
That consecrated it could be
The only Food that grows

(c. 1882)

1670

In Winter in my Room
I came upon a Worm—
Pink, lank and warm—
But as he was a worm
And worms presume
Not quite with him at home—
Secured him by a string
To something neighboring
And went along.

A Trifle afterward
A thing occurred
I'd not believe it if I heard
But state with creeping blood—
A snake with mottles rare
Surveyed my chamber floor
In feature as the worm before
But ringed with power—

The very string with which
I tied him—too
When he was mean and new
That string was there—

I shrank—"How fair you are"!
Propitiation's claw—
"Afraid," he hissed
"Of me"?
"No cordiality"—
He fathomed me—
Then to a Rhythm Slim
Secreted in his Form

As Patterns swim
Projected him.

That time I flew
Both eyes his way
Lest he pursue
Nor ever ceased to run
Till in a distant Town
Towns on from mine
I set me down
This was a dream.

(1914)

Assurance

Last night I slept, and when I woke her kiss
Still floated on my lips. For we had strayed
Together in my dream, through some dim glade,
Where the shy moonbeams scarce dared light our bliss.
The air was dank with dew, between the trees,
The hidden glow-worms kindled and were spent.
Cheek pressed to cheek, the cool, the hot night-breeze
Mingled our hair, our breath, and came and went,
As sporting with our passion. Low and deep
Spake in mine ear her voice: "And didst thou dream,
This could be buried? This could be sleep?
And love be thrall to death! Nay, whatso seem,
Have faith, dear heart; *this is the thing that is!*"
Thereon I woke, and on my lips her kiss.

(1980)

ᗡᗢ

Terminus

Wonderful was the long secret night you gave me, my
    Lover,
Palm to palm, breast to breast in the gloom. The faint
    red lamp,
Flushing with magical shadows the common-place room
    of the inn,
With its dull impersonal furniture, kindled a mystic
    flame
In the heart of the swinging mirror, the glass that has
    seen
Faces innumerous & vague of the endless travelling
    automata,
Whirled down the ways of the world like dust-eddies
    swept through a street,
Faces indifferent or weary, frowns of impatience or pain,
Smiles (if such there were ever) like your smile and mine
    when they met
Here, in this self-same glass, while you helped me to
    loosen my dress,
And the shadow-mouths melted to one, like sea-birds
    that meet in a wave—
Such smiles, yes, such smiles the mirror perhaps has
    reflected;
And the low wide bed, as rutted and worn as a
    high-road,
The bed with its soot-sodden chintz, the grime of its
    brasses,
That has borne the weight of fagged bodies, dust-
    stained, averted in sleep,
The hurried, the restless, the aimless—perchance it has
    also thrilled
With the pressure of bodies ecstatic, bodies like ours,

Seeking each other's souls in the depths of unfathomed
     caresses,
And through the long windings of passion emerging
     again to the stars . . .
Yes, all this through the room, the passive & featureless
     room,
Must have flowed with the rise & fall of the human
     unceasing current;
And lying there hushed in your arms, as the waves of
     rapture receded,
And far down the margin of being we heard the low
     beat of the soul,
I was glad as I thought of those others, the nameless, the
     many,
Who perhaps thus had lain and loved for an hour on the
     brink of the world,
Secret and fast in the heart of the whirlwind of travel,
The shaking and shrieking of trains, the night-long
     shudder of traffic,
Thus, like us they have lain & felt, breast to breast in
     the dark,
The fiery rain of possession descend on their limbs
     while outside
The black rain of midnight pelted the roof of the
     station;
And thus some woman like me, waking alone before
     dawn,
While her lover slept, as I woke & heard the calm stir of
     your breathing,
Some woman has heard as I heard the farewell shriek of
     the trains
Crying good-bye to the city & staggering out into
     darkness,
And shaken at heart has thought: "So must we forth in
     the darkness,
Sped down the fixed rail of habit by the hand of
     implacable fate—
So shall we issue to life, & the rain, & the dull dark
     dawning;

You to the wide flare of cities, with windy garlands and
    shouting,
Carrying to populous places the freight of holiday
    throngs;
I, by waste lands, & stretches of low-skied marsh
To a harbourless wind-bitten shore, where a dull town
    moulders & shrinks,
And its roofs fall in, & the sluggish feet of the hours
Are printed in grass in its streets; & between the
    featureless houses
Languid the town-folk glide to stare at the entering
    train,
The train from which no one descends; till one pale
    evening of winter,
When it halts on the edge of the town, see, the houses
    have turned into grave-stones,
The streets are the grassy paths between the low roofs
    of the dead;
And as the train glides in ghosts stand by the doors of
    the carriages;
And scarcely the difference is felt—yea, such is the life I
    return to . . ."
Thus may another have thought; thus, as I turned may
    have turned
To the sleeping lips at her side, to drink, as I drank
    there, oblivion. . . .

(c. 1909)

❧

The Subverted Flower

She drew back; he was calm;
"It is this that had the power."
And he lashed his open palm
With the tender-headed flower.
He smiled for her to smile,
But she was either blind
Or willfully unkind.
He eyed her for a while
For a woman and a puzzle.
He flicked and flung the flower,
And another sort of smile
Caught up like finger tips
The corners of his lips
And cracked his ragged muzzle.
She was standing to the waist
In goldenrod and brake,
Her shining hair displaced.
He stretched her either arm
As if she made it ache
To clasp her — not to harm;
As if he could not spare
To touch her neck and hair.
"If this has come to us
And not to me alone —"
So she thought she heard him say;
Though with every word he spoke
His lips were sucked and blown
And the effort made him choke
Like a tiger at a bone.
She had to lean away.
She dared not stir a foot,
Lest movement should provoke

The demon of pursuit
That slumbers in a brute.
It was then her mother's call
From inside the garden wall
Made her steal a look of fear
To see if he could hear
And would pounce to end it all
Before her mother came.
She looked and saw the shame:
A hand hung like a paw,
An arm worked like a saw
As if to be persuasive,
An ingratiating laugh
That cut the snout in half,
An eye become evasive.
A girl could only see
That a flower had marred a man,
But what she could not see
Was that the flower might be
Other than base and fetid:
That the flower had done but part,
And what the flower began
Her own too meager heart
Had terribly completed.
She looked and saw the worst.
And the dog or what it was,
Obeying bestial laws,
A coward save at night,
Turned from the place and ran.
She heard him stumble first
And use his hands in flight.
She heard him bark outright.
And oh, for one so young
The bitter words she spit
Like some tenacious bit
That will not leave the tongue.
She plucked her lips for it,
And still the horror clung.
Her mother wiped the foam

From her chin, picked up her comb,
And drew her backward home.

(1942)

AMY LOWELL (1874–1925)

Anticipation

I have been temperate always,
But I am like to be very drunk
With your coming.
There have been times
I feared to walk down the street
Lest I should reel with the wine of you,
And jerk against my neighbours
As they go by.
I am parched now, and my tongue is horrible in my mouth,
But my brain is noisy
With the clash and gurgle of filling wine-cups.

(1914)

from *Lifting Belly*

Kiss my lips. She did.
Kiss my lips again she did.
Kiss my lips over and over and over again she did.
I have feathers.
Gentle fishes.
Do you think about apricots. We find them very beautiful.
It is not alone their color it is their seeds that charm us. We
find it a change.
Lifting belly is so strange.
I came to speak about it.
Selected raisins well then grapes grapes are good.
Change your name.
Question and garden.
It's raining. Don't speak about it.
My baby is a dumpling I want to tell her something.
Wax candles. We have bought a great many wax candles.
Some are decorated. They have not been lighted.
I do not mention roses.
Exactly.
Actually.
Question and butter.
I find the butter very good.
Lifting belly is so kind.
Lifting belly fattily.
Doesn't that astonish you.
You did want me.
Say it again.
Strawberry.
Lifting beside belly.
Lifting kindly belly.
Sing to me I say.
Some are wives not heroes.
Lifting belly merely.

Sing to me I say.

Lifting belly. A reflection.

Lifting belly adjoins more prizes.

Fit to be.

I have fit on a hat.

Have you.

What did you say to excuse me. Difficult paper and scattered.

Lifting belly is so kind.

What shall you say about that. Lifting belly is so kind.

What is a veteran.

A veteran is one who has fought.

Who is the best.

The king and the queen and the mistress.

Nobody has a mistress.

Lifting belly is so kind.

To-day we decided to forgive Nellie.

Anybody can describe dresses.

How do you do what is the news.

Lifting belly is so kind.

Lifting belly exactly.

The king and the prince of Montenegro.

Lifting belly is so kind.

Lifting belly to please me.

Excited.

Excited are you.

I can whistle, the train can whistle we can hear the whistle, the boat whistle. The train is not running to-day. Mary whistle whistle for the whim.

Didn't you say you'd write it better.

Mrs. Vettie. It is necessary to have a Ford.

Yes sir.

Dear Mrs. Vettie. Smile to me.

I am.

Dear Mrs. Vettie never better.

Yes indeed so.

Lifting belly is most kind.

What did I say, that I was a great poet like the English only sweeter.

When I think of this afternoon and the garden I see what you mean.

You are not thinking of the pleasure.

Lifting belly again.

What did I mention when I drew a pansy that pansy and petunia both begin with p.

Lifting belly splendidly.

We have wishes.

Let us say we know it.

Did I say anything about it. I know the tide. We know the title.

Lifting belly is so kind.

We have made no mistake.

The Montenegrin family.

A condition to a wide admiration.

Lifting belly before all.

You don't mean disobedience.

Lifting belly all around.

Eat the little girl I say.

Listen to me. Did you expect it to go back. Why do you do to stop.

What do you do to stop.

What do you do to go on.

I do the same.

Yes wishes. Oh yes wishes.

What do you do to turn a corner.

What do you do to sing.

We don't mention singing.

What do you do to be reformed.

You know.

Yes wishes.

What do you do to measure.

I do it in such a way.

I hope to see them come.

Lifting belly go around.

I was sorry to be blistered.

We were such company.

Did she say jelly.

Jelly my jelly.

Lifting belly is so round.

Big Caesars.
Two Caesars.
Little seize her.
Too.
Did I do my duty.
Did I wet my knife.
No I don't mean whet.
Exactly four teeth.
Little belly is so kind.
What did you say about accepting.
Yes.
Lifting belly another lifting belly.
I question the weather.
It is not necessary.
Lifting belly oh lifting belly in time.
Yes indeed.
Be to me.
Did you say this was this.
Mr. Louis.
Do not mention Mr. Louis.
Little axes.
Yes indeed little axes and rubbers.
This is a description of an automobile.
I understand all about them.
Lifting belly is so kind.
So is whistling.
A great many whistles are shrill.
Lifting belly connects.
Lifting belly again.
Sympathetic blessing.
Not curls.
Plenty of wishes.
All of them fulfilled.
Lifting belly you don't say so.
Climb trees.
Lifting belly has sparks.
Sparks of anger and money.
Lifting belly naturally celebrates.
We naturally celebrate.
Connect me in places.

Lifting belly.
No no don't say that.
Lifting belly oh yes.
Tax this.
Running behind a mountain.
I fly to thee.
Lifting belly.
Shall I chat.
I mean pugilists.
Oh yes trainer.
Oh yes yes.
Say it again to study.
It has been perfectly fed.
Oh yes I do.
Belly alright.
Lifting belly very well.
Lifting belly this.
So sweet.
To me.
Say anything a pudding made of Caesars.
Lobster. Baby is so good to baby.
I correct blushes. You mean wishes.
I collect pearls. Yes and colors.
All colors are dogs. Oh yes Beddlington.
Now I collect songs.
Lifting belly is so nice.
I wrote about it to him.
I wrote about it to her.
Not likely not very likely that they will seize rubber. Not
very likely that they will seize rubber.
Lifting belly yesterday.
And to-day.
And to-morrow.
A train to-morrow.
Lifting belly is so exacting.
Lifting belly asks any more.
Lifting belly captures.
Seating.
Have a swim.
Lifting belly excuses.

Can you swim.
Lifting belly for me.
When this you see remember me.

(1915–1917)

WALLACE STEVENS (1879–1955)

⁓

Peter Quince at the Clavier

I

Just as my fingers on these keys
Make music, so the selfsame sounds
On my spirit make a music, too.

Music is feeling, then, not sound;
And thus it is that what I feel,
Here in this room, desiring you,

Thinking of your blue-shadowed silk,
Is music. It is like the strain
Waked in the elders by Susanna.

Of a green evening, clear and warm,
She bathed in her still garden, while
The red-eyed elders watching, felt

The basses of their beings throb
In witching chords, and their thin blood
Pulse pizzicati of Hosanna.

II

In the green water, clear and warm,
Susanna lay.
She searched
The touch of springs,
And found
Concealed imaginings.
She sighed,
For so much melody.

Upon the bank, she stood
In the cool
Of spent emotions.
She felt, among the leaves,
The dew
Of old devotions.

She walked upon the grass,
Still quavering.
The winds were like her maids,
On timid feet,
Fetching her woven scarves,
Yet wavering.

A breath upon her hand
Muted the night.
She turned—
A cymbal crashed,
And roaring horns.

III

Soon, with a noise like tambourines,
Came her attendant Byzantines.

They wondered why Susanna cried
Against the elders by her side;

And as they whispered, the refrain
Was like a willow swept by rain.

Anon, their lamps' uplifted flame
Revealed Susanna and her shame.

And then, the simpering Byzantines
Fled, with a noise like tambourines.

IV

Beauty is momentary in the mind—
The fitful tracing of a portal;
But in the flesh it is immortal.

The body dies; the body's beauty lives.
So evenings die, in their green going,
A wave, interminably flowing.
So gardens die, their meek breath scenting
The cowl of winter, done repenting.
So maidens die, to the auroral
Celebration of a maiden's choral.

Susanna's music touched the bawdy strings
Of those white elders; but, escaping,
Left only Death's ironic scraping.
Now, in its immortality, it plays
On the clear viol of her memory,
And makes a constant sacrament of praise.

(1915)

∾

Young Sycamore

I must tell you
this young tree
whose round and firm trunk
between the wet

pavement and the gutter
(where water
is trickling) rises
bodily

into the air with
one undulant
thrust half its height—
and then

dividing and waning
sending out
young branches on
all sides—

hung with cocoons
it thins
till nothing is left of it
but two

eccentric knotted
twigs
bending forward
hornlike at the top

(1927)

Sea Holly

Begotten by the meeting of rock with rock,
The mating of rock and rock, rocks gnashing together;
Created so, and yet forgetful, walks
The seaward path, puts up her left hand, shades
Blue eyes, the eyes of rock, to see better
In slanting light the ancient sheep (which kneels
Biting the grass) the while her other hand,
Hooking the wicker handle, turns the basket
Of eggs. The sea is high to-day. The eggs
Are cheaper. The sea is blown from the southwest,
Confused, taking up sand and mud in waves,
The waves break, sluggish, in brown foam, the wind
Disperses (on the sheep and hawthorn) spray,—
And on her cheeks, the cheeks engendered of rock,
And eyes, the colour of rock. The left hand
Falls from the eyes, and undecided slides
Over the left breast on which muslin lightly
Rests, touching the nipple, and then down
The hollow side, virgin as rock, and bitterly
Caresses the blue hip.

           It was for this,
This obtuse taking of the seaward path,
This stupid hearing of larks, this hooking
Of wicker, this absent observation of sheep
Kneeling in harsh sea-grass, the cool hand shading
The spray-stung eyes—it was for this the rock
Smote itself. The sea is higher today,
And eggs are cheaper. The eyes of rock take in
The seaward path that winds toward the sea,
The thistle-prodder, old woman under a bonnet,
Forking the thistles, her back against the sea,

Pausing, with hard hands on the handle, peering
With rock eyes from her bonnet.

                    It was for this,
This rock-lipped facing of brown waves, half sand
And half water, this tentative hand that slides
Over the breast of rock, and into the hollow
Soft side of muslin rock, and then fiercely
Almost as rock against the hip of rock—
It was for this in midnight the rocks met,
And dithered together, cracking and smoking.

                    It was for this
Barren beauty, barrenness of rock that aches
On the seaward path, seeing the fruitful sea,
Hearing the lark of rock that sings, smelling
The rock-flower of hawthorn, sweetness of rock—
It was for this, stone pain in the stony heart,
The rock loved and laboured; and all is lost.

                    (1925)

EDNA ST. VINCENT MILLAY (1892–1950)

I too beneath your moon, almighty Sex,
Go forth at nightfall crying like a cat,
Leaving the lofty tower I laboured at
For birds to foul and boys and girls to vex
With tittering chalk; and you, and the long necks
Of neighbours sitting where their mothers sat
Are well aware of shadowy this and that
In me, that's neither noble nor complex.
Such as I am, however, I have brought
To what it is, this tower; it is my own;
Though it was reared To Beauty, it was wrought
From what I had to build with: honest bone
Is there, and anguish; pride; and burning thought;
And lust is there, and nights not spent alone.

(1939)

E. E. CUMMINGS (1894–1962)

as
we lie side by side
my little breasts become two sharp delightful strutting towers and
i shove hotly the lovingness of my belly against you

your arms are
young;
your arms will convince me,in the complete silence speaking
upon my body
their ultimate slender language.

do not laugh at my thighs.

there is between my big legs a crisp city.
when you touch me
it is Spring in the city;the streets beautifully writhe,
it is for you;do not frighten them,
all the houses terribly tighten
upon your coming:
and they are glad
as you fill the streets of my city with children.

my love you are a bright mountain which feels.
you are a keen mountain and an eager island whose
lively slopes are based always in the me which is shrugging,which is
under you and around you and forever:i am the hugging sea.
O mountain you cannot escape me
your roots are anchored in my silence;therefore O mountain
skilfully murder my breasts,still and always

i will hug you solemnly into me.

(1918–1919)

Sonnets to Some Sexual Organs

I

Female

Mother of Men, and bearded like a male;
Loose lips that smile and smile without a face;
Mistress of vision, paths which cannot fail,
If rightly trod, to save the human race—

O, queenly hole, it is most wisely done
That you like oracles are kept from sight
And only show yourself when one by one
Man's wits have to his blood lost their delight.

So, perfumed high and finely diapered
And coyly hidden in the fat of thighs,
You shall be mystic still, and your absurd
And empty grin shall mock no lover's eyes.

For love of you, for love of you, old hole,
Man made the dream of woman and her soul.

II

Male

O, ludicrous and pensive trinity;
O, jest dependent from the loins of man;
Symbolic pink and white futility,
From which let him escape who thinks he can—

Whether in throbbing hope you raise your head,
One-eyed and hatless, peering from the bush,
Or if you dangle melancholy dead,
A battered hose, long-punished in the push,

It matters not; you are the potent lord,
The hidden spinner of our magic schemes,
The master of the arts, the captain sword,
The source of all our attitudes and dreams.

You lead us, master, sniffing to the hunt,
In quest forever of the perfect cunt.

(1971)

Episode of Hands

The unexpected interest made him flush.
Suddenly he seemed to forget the pain,—
Consented,—and held out
One finger from the others.

The gash was bleeding, and a shaft of sun
That glittered in and out among the wheels,
Fell lightly, warmly, down into the wound.

And as the fingers of the factory owner's son,
That knew a grip for books and tennis
As well as one for iron and leather,—
As his taut, spare fingers wound the gauze
Around the thick bed of the wound,
His own hands seemed to him
Like wings of butterflies
Flickering in sunlight over summer fields.

The knots and notches,—many in the wide
Deep hand that lay in his,—seemed beautiful.
They were like the marks of wild ponies' play,—
Bunches of new green breaking a hard turf.

And factory sounds and factory thoughts
Were banished from him by that larger, quieter hand
That lay in his with the sun upon it.
And as the bandage knot was tightened
The two men smiled into each other's eyes.

(1920)

∾

Desire

Desire to us
Was like a double death,
Swift dying
Of our mingled breath,
Evaporation
Of an unknown strange perfume
Between us quickly
In a naked
Room.

(1947)

KENNETH REXROTH (1905–1982)

from *The Love Poems of Marichiko*

To Marichiko
Kenneth Rexroth

To Kenneth Rexroth
Marichiko

III

Oh the anguish of these secret meetings
In the depth of night,
I wait with the shoji open.
You come late, and I see your shadow
Move through the foliage
At the bottom of the garden.
We embrace—hidden from my family.
I weep into my hands.
My sleeves are already damp.
We make love, and suddenly
The fire watch loom up
With clappers and lantern.
How cruel they are
To appear at such a moment.
Upset by their apparition,
I babble nonsense
And can't stop talking
Words with no connection.

IV

You ask me what I thought about
Before we were lovers.
The answer is easy.

Before I met you
I didn't have anything to think about.

VII

Making love with you
Is like drinking sea water.
The more I drink
The thirstier I become,
Until nothing can slake my thirst
But to drink the entire sea.

IX

You wake me,
Part my thighs, and kiss me.
I give you the dew
Of the first morning of the world.

XIV

On the bridges
And along the banks
Of Kamo River, the crowds
Watch the character "Great"
Burst into red fire on the mountain
And at last die out.
Your arm about me,
I burn with passion.
Suddenly I realize—
It is life I am burning with.
These hands burn,
Your arm about me burns,
And look at the others,
All about us in the crowd, thousands,
They are all burning—
Into embers and then into darkness.
I am happy.
Nothing of mine is burning.

XVI

Scorched with love, the cicada
Cries out. Silent as the firefly,
My flesh is consumed with love.

XXIV

I scream as you bite
My nipples, and orgasm
Drains my body, as if I
Had been cut in two.

XXV

Your tongue thrums and moves
Into me, and I become
Hollow and blaze with
Whirling light, like the inside
Of a vast expanding pearl.

XXVII

As I came from the
Hot bath, you took me before
The horizontal mirror
Beside the low bed, while my
Breasts quivered in your hands, my
Buttocks shivered against you.

XXXII

I hold your head tight between
My thighs, and press against your
Mouth, and float away
Forever, in an orchid
Boat on the River of Heaven.

XXXIII

I cannot forget
The perfumed dusk inside the
Tent of my black hair,
As we awoke to make love
After a long night of love.

XLII

How many lives ago
I first entered the torrent of love,
At last to discover
There is no further shore.
Yet I know I will enter again and again.

(1979)

The Platonic Blow

It was a spring day, a day for a lay, when the air
Smelled like a locker-room, a day to blow or get blown;
Returning from lunch I turned my corner and there
On a near-by stoop I saw him standing alone.

I glanced as I advanced. The clean white T-shirt outlined
A forceful torso: the light-blue denims divulged
Much. I observed the snug curves where they hugged the behind,
I watched the crotch where the cloth intriguingly bulged.

Our eyes met. I felt sick. My knees turned weak.
I couldn't move. I didn't know what to say.
In a blur I hear words, myself like a stranger speak
"Will you come to my room?" Then a husky voice "O. K."

I produced some beer and we talked. Like a little boy
He told me his story. Present address: next door.
Half Polish, half Irish. The youngest. From Illinois.
Profession: mechanic. Name: Bud. Age: twenty-four.

He put down his glass and stretched his bare arms along
The back of my sofa. The afternoon sunlight struck
The blond hairs on the wrist near my head. His chin was strong,
His mouth sucky. I could hardly believe my luck.

And here he was, sitting beside me, legs apart.
I could bear it no longer. I touched the inside of his thigh.
His reply was to move it closer. I trembled, my heart
Thumped and jumped as my fingers went to his fly.

I opened the gap in the flap. I went in there.
I sought for a slit in the gripper shorts that had charge

Of the basket I asked for. I came to warm flesh, then to hair.
I went on. I found what I hoped. I groped. It was large.

He responded to my fondling in a charming, disarming way:
Without a word he unbuckled his belt while I felt.
And lolled back, stretching his legs. His pants fell away.
Carefully drawing it out, I beheld what I held.

The circumcised head was a work of mastercraft
With perfectly bevelled rim, of unusual weight
And the friendliest red. Even relaxed, the shaft
Was of noble dimensions with wrinkles that indicate

Singular powers of extension. For a second or two
It lay there inert, then it suddenly stirred in my hand,
Then paused as if frightened or doubtful of what to do.
And then with a violent jerk began to expand.

By soundless bounds it extended and distended, by quick
Great leaps it rose, it flushed, it rushed to its full size.
Nearly nine inches long and three inches thick,
A royal column, ineffably solemn and wise.

I tested its length with a manual squeeze.
I bunched my fingers and twirled them about the knob.
I stroked it from top to bottom. I got on my knees.
I lowered my head. I opened my mouth for the job.

But he pushed me gently away. He bent down. He unlaced
His shoes. He removed his socks. Stood up. Shed
His pants altogether. Muscles in arm and waist
Rippled as he whipped his T-shirt over his head.

I scanned his tan, enjoyed the contrast of the brown
Trunk against white shorts taut around small
Hips. With a dig and a wriggle he peeled them down.
I tore off my clothes. He faced me, smiling. I saw all.

The gorgeous organ stood stiffly and straightly out
With a slight flare upwards. At each beat of his heart it threw

An odd little nod my way. From the slot of the spout
Extended a drop of transparent viscous goo.

The lair of the hair was fair, the grove of a young man,
A tangle of curls and whorls, luxuriant but couth.
Except for a spur of golden hairs that ran
To the neat navel, the rest of the belly was smooth.

Well-hung, slung from the form of the muscular legs,
The firm vase of sperm like a bulging pear,
Cradling its handsome glands, two herculean eggs,
Swung as he came towards me, shameless, bare.

We aligned mouths. We entwined. All act was clutch,
All fact, contact, the attack and the interlock
Of tongues, the charms of arms. I shook at the touch
Of his fresh flesh, I rocked at the shock of his cock.

Straddling my legs a little I inserted his divine
Person between and closed on it tight as I could.
The upright warmth of his belly lay along mine.
Nude, glued together, for a minute we stood.

I stroked the lobes of his ears, the back of his head
And the broad shoulders. I took bold hold of the compact
Globes of his bottom. We tottered. He fell on the bed.
Lips parted, eyes closed, he lay there, ripe for the act,

Mad to be had, to be felt and smelled. My lips
Explored the adorable masculine tits. My eyes
Assessed the chest. I caressed the athletic hips
And the skim limbs. I approved the grooves of his thighs.

I hugged, I snugged into an armpit. I sniffed
The subtle whiff of its tuft. I lapped up the taste
Of its hot hollow. My fingers began to drift
On a trek of inspection, a leisurely tour of the waist.

Downward in narrowing circles they playfully strayed,
Encroached on his privates like poachers, approached the prick,

But teasingly swerved, retreated from meeting. It betrayed
Its pleading need by a pretty imploring kick.

"Shall I rim you?" I whispered. He shifted his limbs in assent.
Turned on his side and opened his legs, let me pass
To the dark parts behind. I kissed as I went
The great thick cord that ran from his balls to his arse.

Prying the buttocks aside, I nosed my way in
Down the shaggy slopes. I came to the puckered goal.
It was quick to my licking. He pressed his crotch to my chin.
His thighs squirmed as my tongue wormed in his hole.

His sensations yearned for consummation. He untucked
His legs and lay panting, hot as a teen-age boy,
Naked, enlarged, charged, aching to get sucked,
Clawing the sheet, all his pores open to joy.

I inspected his erection. I surveyed his parts with a stare
From scrotum level. Sighting along the underside
Of his cock I looked through the forest of pubic hair
To the range of the chest beyond, rising lofty and wide.

I admired the texture, the delicate wrinkles and the neat
Sutures of the capacious bag. I adored the grace
Of the male genitalia. I raised the delicious meat
Up to my mouth, brought the face of its hard-on to my face.

Slipping my lips around the Byzantine dome of the head.
With the tip of my tongue I caressed the sensitive groove.
He thrilled to the trill. "That's lovely!" he hoarsely said.
"Go on! Go on!" Very slowly I started to move.

Gently, intently, I slid to the massive base
Of his tower of power, paused there a moment down
In the warm moist thicket, then began to retrace
Inch by inch the smooth way to the throbbing crown.

Indwelling excitements swelled at delights to come
As I descended and ascended those thick distended walls.

I grasped his root between my left forefinger and thumb
And with my right hand ticked his heavy, voluminous balls.

I plunged with a rhythmical lunge, steady and slow,
And at every stroke made a corkscrew roll with my tongue.
He soul reeled in the feeling. He whimpered "Oh!"
As I tongued and squeezed and rolled and tickled and swung.

Then I pressed on the spot where the groin is joined to the cock,
Slipped a finger into his arse and massaged him from inside.
The secret sluices of his juices began to unlock.
He melted into what he felt. "O Jesus!" he cried.

Waves of immeasurable pleasures mounted his member in quick
Spasms. I lay still in the notch of his crotch inhaling his sweat.
His ring convulsed around my finger. Into me, rich and thick,
His hot spunk spouted in gouts, spurted in jet after jet.

(1948)

ELIZABETH BISHOP (1911–1979)

"It Is Marvellous . . ."

It is marvellous to wake up together
At the same minute; marvellous to hear
The rain begin suddenly all over the roof,
To feel the air clear
As if electricity had passed through it
From a black mesh of wires in the sky.
All over the roof the rain hisses,
And below, the light falling of kisses.

An electrical storm is coming or moving away;
It is the prickling air that wakes us up.
If lightning struck the house now, it would run
From the four blue china balls on top
Down the roof and down the rods all around us,
And we imagine dreamily
How the whole house caught in a bird-cage of lightning
Would be quite delightful rather than frightening;

And from the same simplified point of view
Of night and lying flat on one's back
All things might change equally easily,
Since always to warn us there must be these black
Electrical wires dangling. Without surprise
The world might change to something quite different,
As the air changes or the lightning comes without our blinking,
Change as our kisses are changing without our thinking.

(1988)

J. V. CUNNINGHAM (1911–1985)

It Was in Vegas

It was in Vegas. Celibate and able
I left the silver dollars on the table
And tried the show. Aloha, baggy pants,
Of course, and then this answer to romance:
Her ass twitching as if it had the fits,
Her gold crotch grinding, her athletic tits,
One clock-, the other counter-clockwise twirling.
It was enough to stop a man from girling.

(1964)

TENNESSEE WILLIAMS (1911–1983)

Life Story

After you've been to bed together for the first time,
without the advantage or disadvantage of any prior acquaintance,
the other party very often says to you,
Tell me about yourself, I want to know all about you,
what's your story? And you think maybe they really and truly do

sincerely want to know your life story, and so you light up
a cigarette and begin to tell it to them, the two of you
lying together in completely relaxed positions
like a pair of rag dolls a bored child dropped on a bed.

You tell them your story, or as much of your story
as time or a fair degree of prudence allows, and they say,
        Oh, oh, oh, oh, oh,
each time a little more faintly, until the oh
is just an audible breath, and then of course

there's some interruption. Slow room service comes up
with a bowl of melting ice cubes, or one of you rises to pee
and gaze at himself with mild astonishment in the bathroom mirror.
And then, the first thing you know, before you've had time
to pick up where you left off with your enthralling life story,
they're telling you *their* life story, exactly as they'd intended to all
        along,

and you're saying, Oh, oh, oh, oh, oh,
each time a little more faintly, the vowel at last becoming
no more than an audible sigh,
as the elevator, halfway down the corridor and a turn to the left,
draws one last, long, deep breath of exhaustion
and stops breathing forever. Then?

Well, one of you falls asleep
and the other one does likewise with a lighted cigarette in his
    mouth,
and that's how people burn to death in hotel rooms.

(1956)

What I See

Lie there, in sweat and dream, I do, and "there"
Is here, my bed, on which I dream
You, lying there, on yours, locked, pouring love,
While I tormented here see in my reins
You, perfectly at climax. And the lion strikes.
I want you with whatever obsessions come—
I wanted your obsession to be mine
But if it is that unknown half-suggested strange
Other figure locked in your climax, then
I here, I want you and the other, want your obsession,
     want
Whatever is locked into you now while I sweat and
     dream.

(1968)

MAY SWENSON (1913–1989)

A New Pair

Like stiff whipped cream in peaks and tufts afloat,
the two on barely gliding waves approach.

One's neck curves back, the whole head to the eyebrows
hides in the wing's whiteness.

The other drifts erect, one dark splayed foot
lifted along a snowy hull.

On thin, transparent platforms of the waves
the pair approach each other, as if without intent.

Do they touch? Does it only seem so to my eyes'
perspective where I stand on shore?

I wish them together, to become one fleece enfolded, proud
vessel of cloud, shape until now unknown.

Tense, I stare and wait, while slow waves carry them
closer. And side does graze creamy side.

One tall neck dips, is laid along the other's back,
at the place where an arm would embrace.

A brief caress. Then both sinuous necks arise,
their paddle feet fall to water. As I stare,
with independent purpose at full sail, they steer apart.

(1985)

ISABELLA STEWART GARDNER (1915–1981)

The Milkman

The door was bolted and the windows of my porch
were screened to keep invaders out, the mesh of rust-
proof wire sieved the elements. Did my throat parch
then sat I at my table there and ate with lust
most chaste, the raw red apples; juice, flesh, rind and core.

One still and summer noon while dining in the sun
I was poulticing my thirst with apples, slaking care,
when suddenly I felt a whir of dread. Soon, soon,
stiff as a bone, I listened for the Milkman's tread.
I heard him softly bang the door of the huge truck
and then his boots besieged my private yard. I tried
to keep my eyes speared to the table, but the suck
of apprehension milked my force. At last he mounted
my backstairs, climbed to the top, and there he stood still
outside the bolted door. The sun's colour fainted.
I felt the horror of his quiet melt me, steal
into my sockets, and seduce me to him from
my dinner. His hand clung round the latch like rubber.
I felt him ooze against the screen and shake the frame.
I had to slide the bolt; and thus I was the robber
of my porch. Breathing smiling shape of fright,
the Milkman made his entrance; insistent donor,
he held in soft bleached hands the bottled sterile fruit,
and gave me this fatal, this apostate dinner.

Now in winter I have retreated from the porch
into the house and the once red apples rot where
I left them on the table. Now if my throat parch
for fruit the Milkman brings a quart for my despair.

(1955)

RUTH STONE (BORN 1915)

❧

Coffee and Sweet Rolls

When I remember the dingy hotels
where we lay reading Baudelaire,
your long elegant fingers, the nervous ritual
of your cigarette; you, a young poet working
in the steel mills; me, married
to a dull chemical engineer.
Fever of having nothing to lose;
no luggage, a few books, the streetcar.
In the manic shadow of Hitler, the guttural
monotony of war; often just enough money
for the night. Rising together in the clanking
elevators to those rooms where we lay like embryos;
helpless in the desire to be completed;
to be issued out into the terrible world.

All night, sighing and waking, insatiable.
At daylight, counting our change, you would go for coffee.
Then, lying alone, I heard the sirens,
the common death of everything and again
the little girl I didn't know
all in white in a white casket;
the boy I once knew, smashed with his motorcycle
into the pavement, and what was said,
"made a wax figure for his funeral,"
came into me. I had never touched the dead.
Always the lock unclicked and you were back,
our breakfast in a paper sack.
What I waited for was the tremor in your voice.
In those rooms with my eyes half open,
I memorized for that austere and silent woman
who waited in the future,
who for years survived on this fiction;

so even now I can see you standing thin and naked,
the shy flush of your rising cock pointed toward heaven,
as you pull down the dark window shade.

(1995)

THOMAS McGRATH (1916–1990)

from *Letter to an Imaginary Friend*

Sweet Jesus at morning the queenly women of our youth!
The monumental creatures of our summer lust!
Sweet fantastic darlings, as full of juice as plums,
Pneumatic and backless as a functional dream
Where are ye now?
Where were ye then, indeed?

Walking three-legged in the sexual haze,
Drifting toward the Lion on the bosomy hills of summer,
In the hunting light, the marmoreal bulge of the moon,
I wooed them barebacked in the saddling heat.

First was Inez, her face a looney fiction,
Her bottom like concrete and her wrestling arms;
Fay with breasts as hard as hand grenades
(Whose father's shot gun dozed behind the door),
Barefooted Rose, found in the bottom lands
(We laid the flax as flat as forty horses,
The blue bells showering); Amy with her long hair
Drawn in mock modesty between long legs;
And Sandy with her car, who would be driving and do it;
And June who would roll you as in a barrel down hill—
The Gaelic torture; Gin with her snapping trap,
The heliotropic quim: locked in till daybreak;
Literary Esther, who could fox your copy,
And the double Gladys, one blonde, one black.

O great kingdom of Fuck! And myself: plenipotentiary!
Under the dog star's blaze, in the high rooms of the moonlight,
In the doze and balance of the wide noon,
I hung my pennant from the top of the windy mast:
Jolly Roger sailing the want-not seas of the summers.
And under the coupling of the wheeling night

Muffled in flesh and clamped to the sweaty pelt
Of Blanche or Betty, threshing the green baroque
Stacks of the long hay—the burrs stuck in our crotch,
The dust thick in our throats so we sneezed in spasm—
Or flat on the floor, or the back seat of a car,
Or a groaning trestle table in the Methodist Church basement,
And far in the fields, and high in the hills, and hot
And quick in the roaring cars: by the bridge, by the river,
In Troop Nine's dank log cabin where the Cheyenne flows:
By light, by dark, up on the roof, in the celler,
In the rattling belfry where the bats complained,
Or backed against trees, or against the squealing fences,
Or belly to belly with no place to lie down
In the light of the dreaming moon.

(1962)

ROBERT DUNCAN (1919–1988)

The Torso (Passage 18)

Most beautiful!   the red-flowering eucalyptus,
  the madrone, the yew

 Is he . . .

So thou wouldst smile, and take me in thine arms
The sight of London to my exiled eyes
Is as Elysium to a new-come soul

  If he be Truth
  I would dwell in the illusion of him

His hands unlocking from chambers of my male body

  such an idea in man's image

rising tides that sweep me towards him

   . . . *homosexual*?

   and at the treasure of his mouth

  pour forth my soul

   his soul commingling

I thought a Being more than vast, His body leading
  into Paradise, his eyes
   quickening a fire in me a trembling

  hieroglyph: At the root of the neck

the clavicle, for the neck is the stem of the great artery
upward into his head that is beautiful

At the rise of the pectoral muscles

the nipples, for the breasts are like sleeping fountains of
feeling in man, waiting above the beat of his heart,
shielding the rise and fall of his breath, to be
awakend

At the axis of his mid riff

the navel, for in the pit of his stomach the chord from
which first he was fed has its temple

At the root of the groin

the pubic hair, for the torso is the stem in which the man
flowers forth and leads to the stamen of flesh in which
his seed rises

a wave of need and desire   over taking me

cried out my name

(This was long ago.   It was another life)

and said,

What do you want of me?

I do not know, I said.   I have fallen in love.   He
has brought me into heights and depths my heart
would fear   without him.   His look

pierces my side   •   fire eyes   •

I have been waiting for you, he said:
I know what you desire

you do not yet know   but through me   •

And I am with you everywhere.   In your falling

I have fallen from a high place.   I have raised myself

from darkness in your   rising

wherever you are

my hand in your hand   seeking   the locks, the keys

I am there.   Gathering me, you gather

your Self   •

For my Other is not a woman but a man

the King upon whose bosom let me lie.

(1968)

Hunk of Rock

Nina was the hardest of them
all,
the worst woman I had known
up to that moment
and I was sitting in front of
my secondhand black and white
tv
watching the news
when I heard a suspicious
sound in the kitchen
and I ran out there
and saw her with
a full bottle of whiskey —
a 5th —
and she had it and
was headed for the back porch
door
but I caught her and
grabbed at the bottle.
"give me that bottle, you
fucking whore!"
and we wrestled for the
bottle
and let me tell you
she gave me a good fight
for it
but
I got it away from her
and I told her to
get her ass out of
there.
she lived in the same place
in the back
upstairs.

I locked the door
took the bottle and a
glass
went out to the couch
sat down and
opened the bottle and
poured myself a good
one.

I shut off the tv and
sat there
thinking about what a
hard number
Nina was.
I came up with
at least
a dozen lousy things
she had done
to me.

what a whore.
what a hunk of rock.

I sat there drinking
the whiskey
and wondering
what I was doing
with Nina.

then there was a
knock on the
door.
it was Nina's friend,
Helga.

"where's Nina?"
she asked.

"she tried to steal
my whiskey, I

ran her ass
out of here."

"she said to meet
her here."

"what for?"

"she said me and her
were going to do it
in front of you
for $50."

"$25."

"she said $50."

"well, she's not
here . . . want a
drink?"

"sure . . ."

I got Helga a glass
poured her a
whiskey.
she took a
hit.

"maybe," she said,
"I ought to go get
Nina."

"I don't want to see
her."

"why not?"

"she's a whore."

Helga finished her
drink and I poured
her another.

she took a
hit.

"Benny calls me a
whore, I'm no
whore."

Benny was the guy
she was shacked
with.

"I know you're no
whore, Helga."

"thanks. Ain't ya got no
music?"

"just the radio . . ."

she saw it
got up
turned it
on.
some music came
blaring out.

Helga began to
dance
holding her whiskey
glass in one
hand.
she wasn't a good
dancer
she looked
ridiculous.

she stopped
drained her drink
rolled her glass along the
rug

then ran toward
me
dropped to her knees
unzipped me
and then
she was down
there
doing tricks.

I drained my
drink
poured another.

she was
good.
she had a college
degree
some place back
East.

"get it, Helga, get
it!"

there was a loud
knock
on the front
door.

"HANK, IS HELGA
THERE?"

"WHO?"

"HELGA!"

"JUST A MINUTE!"

"THIS IS NINA, I WAS
SUPPOSED TO MEET
HELGA HERE, WE HAVE A
LITTLE SURPRISE FOR
YOU!"

"YOU TRIED TO STEAL
MY WHISKEY, YOU
WHORE!"

"HANK, LET ME
IN!"

"get it, Helga, get
it!"

"HANK!"

"Helga, you fucking whore . . .
Helga! Helga! Helga!!"

I pulled away and
got up.

"let her in."

I went to the
bathroom.

when I came out they
were both sitting there
drinking and smoking
laughing about
something.
then they
saw me.

"50 bucks," said Nina.

"25 bucks," I said.

"we won't do it
then."

"don't then."

Nina inhaled
exhaled.
"all right, you
cheap bastard, 25
bucks!"

Nina stood up and
began taking her
clothes off.

she was the hardest
of them
all.

Helga stood up and
began taking her
clothes off.

I poured a
drink.
"sometimes I wonder
what the hell is
going on
around here," I
said.

"don't worry about
it, Daddy, just
get with it!"

"just what am I
supposed to
do?"

"just do
whatever the fuck
you feel
like doing,"
said Nina
her big ass
blazing
in the
lamplight.

(1992)

∿

Assignment

"Then write," she said. "By all means, if that's
   how you feel about it. Write poems.
Write about the recurved arcs of my breasts
   joined in an angle at my nipples, how
the upper curve tilts toward the sky and the lower
   reverses sharply back into my torso,
write about how my throat rises from the supple
   hinge of my collarbones proudly so to speak
with the coin-sized hollow at the center, write
   of the perfect arch of my jaw when I hold
my head back—these are the things in which I too
   take delight—write how my skin is
fine like a cover of snow but warm and soft and
   fitted to me perfectly, write the *volupté*
of soap frothing in my curling crotch-hair, write
   the tight parabola of my vulva that re-
sembles a braided loop swung from a point,
   write the two dapples of light on the backs
of my knees, write my ankles so neatly turning
   in their sockets to deploy all the sweet
bones of my feet, write how when I am aroused
   I sway like a cobra and make sounds
of sucking with my mouth and brush my nipples
   with the tips of my left-hand fingers, and then
write how all this is continually pre-existing in my
   thought and how I effect it in myself
by my will, which you are not permitted to under-
   stand. Do this. Do it in pleasure and with
devotion, and don't worry about time. I won't
   need what you've done until you finish."

(1991)

A Late Aubade

You could be sitting now in a carrel
Turning some liver-spotted page,
Or rising in an elevator-cage
Toward Ladies' Apparel.

You could be planting a raucous bed
Of salvia, in rubber gloves,
Or lunching through a screed of someone's loves
With pitying head,

Or making some unhappy setter
Heel, or listening to a bleak
Lecture on Schoenberg's serial technique.
Isn't this better?

Think of all the time you are not
Wasting, and would not care to waste,
Such things, thank God, not being to your taste.
Think what a lot

Of time, by woman's reckoning,
You've saved, and so may spend on this,
You who had rather lie in bed and kiss
Than anything.

It's almost noon, you say? If so,
Time flies, and I need not rehearse
The rosebuds-theme of centuries of verse.
If you *must* go,

Wait for a while, then slip downstairs
And bring us up some chilled white wine,

And some blue cheese, and crackers, and some fine
Ruddy-skinned pears.

(1969)

꙳

A photograph

shows you in a London
room: books, a painting,
your smile, a silky
tie, a suit. And more.
It looks so like you
and I see it every day
(here, on my desk)
which I don't you. Last
Friday night was grand.
We went out, we came
back, we went wild. You
slept. Me too. The pup
woke you and you dressed
and walked him. When
you left, I was sleeping.
When I woke there was
just time to make the
train to a country dinner
and talk about ecstasy.
Which I think comes in
two sorts: that which you
know "Now I'm ecstatic"
like my strange scream
last Friday night. And
another kind, that you
know only in retrospect:
"Why, that joy I felt
and didn't think about
when his feet were in
my lap, or when I looked
down and saw his slanty
eyes shut, that too was
ecstasy. Nor is there

necessarily a downer from
it." Do I believe in
the perfectibility of
man? Strangely enough,
(I've known un-
happiness enough) I
do. I mean it,
I really do believe
future generations can
live without the in-
tervals of anxious
fear we know between our
bouts and strolls of
ecstasy. The struck ball
finds the pocket. You
smile some years back
in London, I have
known ecstasy and calm:
haven't you, too? Let's
try to understand, my
handsome friend who
wears his nose awry.

(1974)

❧

Summer Storm

In that so sudden summer storm they tried
Each bed, couch, closet, carpet, car-seat, table,
Both river banks, five fields, a mountain side,
Covering as much ground as they were able.

A lady, coming on them in the dark
In a white fixture, wrote to the newspapers
Complaining of the statues in the park.
By Cupid, but they cut some pretty capers!

The envious oxen in still rings would stand
Ruminating. Their sweet incessant plows
I think had changed the contours of the land
And made two modest conies move their house.

God rest them well, and firmly shut the door.
Now they are married Nature breathes once more.

(1949)

2nd Tale: Return

the oldest one and his sister and brother were
lost and he thought, telling a story
will keep fear away.   so he began

the right path is further to your left
where the well is.   and he looked
into the water and the water looked
back.   now it is certain that water
is a magical substance.   it will drink
up all things.   and I am told this is
most like love, who stood near the
high way, and because it is one of
the few bare places the world has
ever known, love asked directions,
but the high way ran on.   now it is
certain that the high way is a magical
substance,   it will lead inside the
shape of things.   and I am told this
is most like love, who has an amazing
ability to surprise travellers.   love
asked the first hitch-hiker to spend
the night with him at the side of the
high way, but the hiker went on.   now
it is certain that a hitch-hiker is
a magical substance which moves along.
and I am told this is most like love,
who has an amazing ability to pass on.
love, then, was quite alone the next
morning, and he stood stock-still
trying to understand, because in the
bright sun, the high way appeared to go
straight on without curves, turn-offs
or junctions into a kind of watery

air.   the rule is, walk on the left
side facing traffic if you don't want
to be killed.   this love did
until after a very long time, he
entered the watery air, which I
remember, is when

they were found

(1969)

❧

To Orgasms

You've never really settled down
Have you, orgasms?
Restless, roving, and not funny
In any way
You change consciousness
Directly, not
Shift of gears
But changing cars
Is more like it. I said my prayers
Ate lunch, read books, and had you.
Someone was there, later, to join me and you
In our festivity, a woman named N.
She said oh we shouldn't do
This I replied oh we should
We did and had you
After you I possess this loveable
Person and she possesses me
There is no more we can do
Until the phone rings
And then we start to plan for you again
And it is obvious
Life may be centered in you
I began to think that every day
Was just one of the blossoms
On the infinitely blossoming
Tree of life
When it was light out we'd say
Soon it will be dark
And when it was dark
We'd say soon it will be light
And we had you.
Sometimes
We'd be sitting at the table

Thinking of you
Or of something related to you
And smiled at other times
Might worry
We read a lot of things about you
Some seemed wrong
It seemed
Puzzling that we had you
Or rather that you
Could have us, in a way,
When you wished to
Though
We had to wish so too
Ah, like what a wild person
To have in the Berkeley apartment!
If anyone knew
That you were there! But they must have known!
You rampaged about we tried to keep you secret.
I mentioned you to no one.
What would there be to say?
That every night or every day
You turned two persons into stone
Hit by dynamite and rocked them till they rolled,
Just about, from bed to floor
And then leaped up and got back into bed
And troubled you no more
For an hour or a day at a time.

(2000)

∾

Their Sex Life

One failure on
Top of another

(1990)

PAUL BLACKBURN (1926–1971)

The Once-Over

The tanned blond
                in the green print sack
in the center of the subway car
                        standing
tho there are seats
                has had it from
1   teen-age hood
1   lesbian
1   envious housewife
4   men over fifty
(& myself),   in short
                   the contents of this half of the car

             Our notations are :
long legs, long waists, high breasts (no bra), long
neck, the model slump
                the handbag drape & how the skirt
cuts in under a very handsome
                     set of cheeks
'stirring dull roots with spring rain' , sayeth the preacher

           Only a stolid young man
with a blue business suit and the New York Times
does not know he is being assaulted

So.
She has us and we her
all the way to downtown Brooklyn
Over the tunnel and through the bridge
                to DeKalb Avenue we go
all very chummy

She stares at the number over the door
                                and gives no sign
Yet the sign is on her

(1958–1960)

∽

Love Poem on Theme by Whitman

I'll go into the bedroom silently and lie down between the bridegroom and th
    bride,
those bodies fallen from heaven stretched out waiting naked and restless,
arms resting over their eyes in the darkness,
bury my face in their shoulders and breasts, breathing their skin,
and stroke and kiss neck and mouth and make back be open and known,
legs raised up crook'd to receive, cock in the darkness driven tormented and
    attacking
rouse up from hole to itching head,
bodies locked shuddering naked, hot lips and buttocks screwed into each othe
and eyes, eyes glinting and charming, widening into looks and abandon,
and moans of movement, voices, hands in air, hands between thighs,
hands in moisture on softened hips, throbbing contraction of bellies
till the white come flow in the swirling sheets,
and the bride cry for forgiveness, and the groom be covered with tears of
    passion and compassion,
and I rise up from the bed replenished with last intimate gestures and kisses of
    farewell—
all before the mind wakes, behind shades and closed doors in a darkened hous
where the inhabitants roam unsatisfied in the night,
nude ghosts seeking each other out in the silence.

(1963)

∽

Peeled Wands

Peeled wands lead on the pedophile. Give me
Experience—and your limbs the prize.
Too scarred and seasoned for mere jeopardy
Ever now to fell them, trunk and thighs
Rampant among sheet lightning and the gruff
Thunderclap be our shelter. Having both
Outstripped the ax-women, enough
Uneasy glances backward! Nothing loath!
Roving past initial bliss and pain
Visited upon you, I have gone bare
Into the thicket of your kiss, and there
Licked from that sly old hermit tongue—
Life's bacon not yet cured when we were young—
Eternal oaths it swore with a salt-grain.

(1988)

FRANK O'HARA (1926–1966)

To the Harbormaster

I wanted to be sure to reach you;
though my ship was on the way it got caught
in some moorings. I am always tying up
and then deciding to depart. In storms and
at sunset, with the metallic coils of the tide
around my fathomless arms, I am unable
to understand the forms of my vanity
or I am hard alee with my Polish rudder
in my hand and the sun sinking. To
you I offer my hull and the tattered cordage
of my will. The terrible channels where
the wind drives me against the brown lips
of the reeds are not all behind me. Yet
I trust the sanity of my vessel; and
if it sinks, it may well be in answer
to the reasoning of the eternal voices,
the waves which have kept me from reaching you.

(1954)

DAVID WAGONER (BORN 1926)

❧

Trying to Write a Poem While the Couple
in the Apartment Overhead Make Love

She's like a singer straying slowly off-key
          While trying too hard to remember the words to a song
                    Without words, and her accompanist
Is metronomically dead set
          To sustain her pitch and tempo, and meanwhile
                    Under their feathers and springs, under their carpet,
Under my own ceiling, I try to go on
          Making something or other out of nothing
                    But those missing words, whose rhythm is only
Predictable for unpredictable moments
          And then erratic, unforeseeable even
                    At its source where it ought to be abundantly,
Even painfully clear. A song is a series of vowels
          Interrupted and shaped by harder consonants
                    And silence, and gifted singers say, if you can
Pronounce words and remember how to breathe,
          You can sing. Although I know some words by heart
                    And think I know how to breathe (even down here
At work alone) and may be able sometimes
          To write some of them down, right now it seems
                    Improbable they'll have anything much like
The permissive diction, the mounting cadences,
          Now, or then or now again the suspended
                    Poise, the drift backward, the surprise
Of the suddenly almost soundless catch
          Of the caught breath, the quick
                    Loss of support
Which wasn't lost at all as it turns out
          But found again and even again
                    Somewhere, in midair, far, far above me.

(2006)

91

GALWAY KINNELL (BORN 1927)

◠

Last Gods

She sits naked on a rock
a few yards out in the water.
He stands on the shore,
also naked, picking blueberries.
She calls. He turns. She opens
her legs showing him her great beauty,
and smiles, a bow of lips
seeming to tie together
the ends of the earth.
Splashing her image
to pieces, he wades out
and stands before her, sunk
to the anklebones in leaf-mush
and bottom-slime—the intimacy
of the visible world. He puts
a berry in its shirt
of mist into her mouth.
She swallows it. He puts in another.
She swallows it. Over the lake
two swallows whim, juke, jink,
and when one snatches
an insect they both whirl up
and exult. He is swollen
not with ichor but with blood.
She takes him and sucks him
more swollen. He kneels, opens
the dark, vertical smile
linking heaven with the underearth
and licks her smoothest flesh more smooth.
On top of the rock they join.
Somewhere a frog moans, a crow screams.
The hair of their bodies
startles up. They cry

in the tongue of the last gods,
who refused to go,
chose death, and shuddered
in joy and shattered in pieces,
bequeathing their cries
into the human mouth. Now in the lake
two faces float, looking up
at a great maternal pine whose branches
open out in all directions
explaining everything.

(1990)

DONALD HALL (BORN 1928)

When I Was Young

When I was young and sexual
    I looked forward to a cool Olympian age
for release from my obsessions.
    Ho, ho, ho. At sixty the body's one desire

sustains my pulse, not to mention
    my groin, as much as it ever did, if not quite
so often. When I gaze at your
    bottom as you bend gardening, or at your breasts,

or at your face with its helmet
    of sensuous hair, or at your eyes proposing
the text of our next encounter,
    my attention departs from history, baseball,

food, poetry, and deathless fame.
    Let us pull back the blanket, slide off our
bluejeans, assume familiar positions,
    and celebrate lust in Mortality Mansions.

(1993)

ANNE SEXTON (1928–1974)

December 11th

Then I think of you in bed,
your tongue half chocolate, half ocean,
of the houses that you swing into,
of the steel wool hair on your head,
of your persistent hands and then
how we gnaw at the barrier because we are two.

How you come and take my blood cup
and link me together and take my brine.
We are bare. We are stripped to the bone
and we swim in tandem and go up and up
the river, the identical river called Mine
and we enter together. No one's alone.

(1967)

RICHARD HOWARD (BORN 1929)

Move Still, Still So

for Sanford Friedman

> Now that I am nearly sixty, I venture to do very
> unconventional things.
> > —Lewis Carroll

1925

. . . bothers me, Doctor, more than the rest,
            more than anything
            I've told you so far—
anything, that is, I could tell you.
            You see, I have this
            feeling, actually
a need . . . I don't know what to call it—yes,
            that's right, *tendency*:
            you know what I mean,
you always know, I suppose that's why
            I'm here at all or
            why I keep coming
back to you when nothing ever seems
            to change . . . I have this
            "tendency" to lie
perfectly still when he wants me to
            let him inside me,
            all of a sudden
I turn passive—how I hate that word!
            I mean I don't feel
            anything is wrong,
but it always happens, just before . . .
            I suppose nothing
            private is really

shocking, so long as it remains yours,
                        but I wish I knew
                        if other women
felt this way. I mean, it seems as if
                        once he's in there I'm
                        waiting for something.
The stillness bothers me. Why can't I
                        accept it? Not what
                        he's doing there, but
the stillness: I can't bear it. Why is that?

1895

> *And was it my fault*
> *it rained Gladyses*
> *and globes? Quite right of Mrs. Grundy,*
> *sending you to bed*
> *one whole day before*
> *your usual time, and since you broke*
> *the window, making*
> *you mend it yourself*
> *with a needle and thread . . . Now, Gladys,*
> *don't fidget so much,*
> *listen to what I say;*
> *I know ways of fixing a restless*
> *child for photographs:*
> *I wedge her, standing,*
> *into the corner of a room, or*
> *if she's lying down,*
> *into the angle*
> *of a sofa. Gladys child, look here*
> *into the lens, and*
> *I'll tell you something . . .*

All these years, Doctor, and I never
                        knew: was I having
                        it or wasn't I?
What I thought I was supposed to have
                        wasn't what *he* thought
                        I should be having,

and to this day I don't think he knows,
　　　　　　or any man knows—
　　　　　　do *you* know, Doctor?
Does it matter if you know or not?
　　　　　　How could a man know—
　　　　　　how or even when
a woman has such things for herself.
　　　　　　Men all imagine
　　　　　　it's the same as theirs,
and of course they think there's only one . . .

　　　　　　　. . . *No you're not. Boredom*
　　　　　　　is something inside
　　　　　　　people, not anything from outside.
　　　　　　　To borrow a word
　　　　　　　from Mrs. Grundy,
　　　　　　　there must be a knot tied in the thread
　　　　　　　before we can sew.
　　　　　　　Your pose is my knot,
　　　　　　　and this camera my way to sew . . .
　　　　　　　Did you ever see
　　　　　　　a needle so huge?
　　　　　　　Of course, having such a thing at home
　　　　　　　is preposterous:
　　　　　　　it is by having
　　　　　　　preposterous possessions that one can
　　　　　　　keep them at arm's length . . .

　　　　　　Before it happens
I don't move, almost not breathing at all,
　　　　　　and I think it's *that,*
　　　　　　the lack of response
he gets discouraged by. He thinks I'm
　　　　　　dead. I wouldn't mind
　　　　　　letting on, Doctor,
but if it happens I just can't speak—
　　　　　　I can't even move.
　　　　　　He thinks it happens
only when I pretend it happens . . .

98

Now that I've made friends
with a real Princess,
I don't intend ever to speak to
any more children
who haven't titles;
but perhaps you have a title, dear,
and you don't know it.
I'm cantankerous,
but not about that sort of thing—about
cooking and grammar
and dresses and dogs . . .

Sometimes I pretend—to save his pride
and prevent a row.
It seems politer,
that way: why be rude about such things?

Now try it a few
minutes like that, child.
Lovely, lovely—one hardly sees why
this little princess
should ever need be
covered up by dreadful crinolines.
Much better that way.
Princess Perdita,
have I told you about her, Gladys?
the one in the Tale
from Shakespeare, who thought
she was a shepherdess, when in fact
she was a real live
princess all the time!

It can happen, and it does, without
tremendous effort,
but unless I take
control and make it the way I want,
it won't work at all . . .
At a certain point
I have to stop trying to fool him

and focus all my
forces on myself.
There must be a feeling that the waves
will come to a crest
—higher waves. Doctor,
sometimes it seems like too much trouble . . .

When the prince saw her—
not doing anything,
just being herself, singing a song
and dancing a bit
at the sheep-shearing,
you know what he told her? Now listen!
What you do, *he said,*
not even guessing
she was a princess, and Perdita
not knowing either,
still betters what is done. When you speak
I'd have you do it ever, when you sing
I'd have you buy and sell so, so give alms,
and for the ordering of your affairs,
to sing them too. When you do dance, I wish you
a wave of the sea, that you might ever do
nothing but that, move still, still so,
and own no other function . . .

Of course it's entirely personal—
there's no way to share
what happens to me,
but I like it that he's there. I always
want to keep my eyes
open, I do try
to make myself feel that much closer
to him, but meanwhile
all I'm conscious of—
the only thing, to tell the truth, is
my own pleasure. There!
That time I said it,
my own pleasure: that is what it is!

And you'll see, Gladys,
that's what photographs
can do, make you a wave of the sea
that you might ever
do nothing but that . . .
So very soon the child-face is gone
forever, sometimes
it is not even
there in children — *hired models are*
plebeian, they have
thick ankles and tend
to be heavy, which I cannot admire.
And of course I must
have little girls, you know
I do not admire naked little boys
in pictures — they seem
to need clothes, always,
whereas one hardly sees why the forms
of little girls should
ever be covered.

I can't make it happen without the right
                    imagining. Sometimes
                    I can't bring it off
and I cast around in my mind for
                    proper images —
                    rather improper,
I'm afraid. I may manage to keep
                    high and dry by day
                    but with the last light
I venture into the water, all
                    that white froth fainting
                    out into darkness —
as if the world had become one wave . . .

           Stockings, even these
           lovely ones, seem to me
           such a pity when a child like you has
           (as is not always
           the case) well-shaped calves.

Yes, that's it. I think we might venture
to face Mrs. Grundy
to the extent of
making a fairy's clothes transparent?
I think Mrs. G
might be fairly well
content to find a fairy dressed at all . . .

I know it isn't
supposed to matter,
but whoever said it wasn't so
important for women
must have been a man!

There we are, ready. Now Gladys, dear,
I want you to lie
still, perfectly still.
I'll help you do it, but the impulse
must be your own. Three
minutes of perfect
stillness will do for both you and me . . .

I always feel cheated whenever
it happens to him
and not to me too.
I treasure those glimpses of the waves
and the high white foam.
I am suspended
before they fall. Doctor, what happens
in that one moment
of timeless suspense?
I feel cast up, out of life, held there
and then down, broken
on the rocks, tossed back,
part of the ebb and the flow. Doctor,
would you mind if I
just lay here, quite still
for a moment? Just this one time, still . . .

(1984)

102

ADRIENNE RICH (BORN 1929)

(The Floating Poem, Unnumbered)

Whatever happens with us, your body
will haunt mine—tender, delicate
your lovemaking, like the half-curled frond
of the fiddlehead fern in forests
just washed by sun. Your traveled, generous thighs
between which my whole face has come and come—
the innocence and wisdom of the place my tongue has found there—
the live, insatiate dance of your nipples in my mouth—
your touch on me, firm, protective, searching
me out, your strong tongue and slender fingers
reaching where I had been waiting years for you
in my rose-wet cave—whatever happens, this is.

(1978)

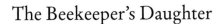

The Beekeeper's Daughter

A garden of mouthings. Purple, scarlet-speckled, black
The great corollas dilate, peeling back their silks.
Their musk encroaches, circle after circle,
A well of scents almost too dense to breathe in.
Hieratical in your frock coat, maestro of the bees,
You move among the many-breasted hives,

My heart under your foot, sister of a stone.

Trumpet-throats open to the beaks of birds.
The Golden Rain Tree drips its powders down.
In these little boudoirs streaked with orange and red
The anthers nod their heads, potent as kings
To father dynasties. The air is rich.
Here is a queenship no mother can contest—

A fruit that's death to taste: dark flesh, dark parings.

In burrows narrow as a finger, solitary bees
Keep house among the grasses. Kneeling down
I set my eye to a hole-mouth and meet an eye
Round, green, disconsolate as a tear.
Father, bridegroom, in this Easter egg
Under the coronal of sugar roses

The queen bee marries the winter of your year.

(1959)

JOHN UPDIKE (BORN 1932)

∾

Fellatio

It is beautiful to think
that each of these clean secretaries
at night, to please her lover, takes
a fountain into her mouth
and lets her insides, drenched in seed,
flower into landscapes:
meadows sprinkled with baby's breath,
hoarse twiggy woods, birds dipping, a multitude
of skies containing clouds, plowed earth stinking
of its upturned humus, and small farms each
with a silver silo.

(1964)

MARK STRAND (BORN 1934)

The Couple

The scene is a midtown station.
    The time is 3 a.m.
Jane is alone on the platform,
    Humming a requiem.

She leans against the tiles.
    She rummages in her purse
For something to ease a headache
    That just keeps getting worse.

She went to a boring party,
    And left without her date.
Now she's alone on the platform,
    And the trains are running late.

The subway station is empty,
    Seedy, sinister, gray.
Enter a well-dressed man
    Slowly heading Jane's way.

The man comes up beside her:
    "Excuse me, my name is John.
I hope I haven't disturbed you.
    If I have, then I'll be gone.

"I had a dream last night
    That I would meet somebody new.
After twenty-four hours of waiting,
    I'm glad she turned out to be you."

Oh where are the winds of morning?
    Oh where is love at first sight?

A man comes out of nowhere.
    Maybe he's Mr. Right.

How does one find the answer,
    If one has waited so long?
A man comes out of nowhere,
    He's probably Mr. Wrong.

Jane imagines the future,
    And almost loses heart.
She sees herself as Europe
    And John as Bonaparte.

They walk to the end of the platform.
    They stumble down to the tracks.
They stand among the wrappers
    And empty cigarette packs.

The wind blows through the tunnel.
    They listen to the sound.
The way it growls and whistles
    Holds them both spellbound.

Jane stares into the dark:
    "It's a wonder sex can be good
When most of the time it comes down to
    Whether one shouldn't or should."

John looks down at his watch:
    "I couldn't agree with you more,
And often it raises the question—
    'What are you saving it for?'"

They kneel beside each other
    As if they were in a trance,
Then Jane lifts up her dress
    And John pulls down his pants.

Everyone knows what happens,
    Or what two people do

When one is on top of the other
　　Making a great to-do.

The wind blows through the tunnel
　　Trying to find the sky.
Jane is breathing her hardest,
　　And John begins to sigh:

"I'm a Princeton professor.
　　God knows what drove me to this.
I have a wife and family;
　　I've known marital bliss.

"But things were turning humdrum,
　　And I felt I was being false.
Every night in our bedroom
　　I wished I were someplace else."

What is the weather outside?
　　What is the weather within
That drives these two to excess
　　And into the arms of sin?

They are the children of Eros.
　　They move, but not too fast.
They want to extend their pleasure,
　　They want the moment to last.

Too bad they cannot hear us.
　　Too bad we can't advise.
Fate that brought them together
　　Has yet another surprise.

Just as they reach the utmost
　　Peak of their endeavor,
An empty downtown local
　　Separates them forever.

An empty downtown local
　　Screams through the grimy air

A couple dies in the subway;
   Couples die everywhere.

(1990)

Dinner at George & Katie Schneeman's

She was pretty swacked by the time she
Put the spaghetti & meatballs into the orgy pasta
     bowl—There was mixed salt & pepper in the
"Tittie-tweak" pasta bowl—We drank some dago red
     from glazed girlie demi-tasse cups—after
which we engaged in heterosexual intercourse, mutual
     masturbation, fellatio, & cunnilingus. For
dessert we stared at a cupboard full of art critic
     friends, sgraffitoed into underglazes on vases. We did
have a very nice time.

(1982)

Conjugal

A man is bending his wife.
He is bending her around something that she has bent herself around. She is around it, bent as he has bent her.

He is convincing her. It is all so private.

He is bending her around the bedpost. No, he is bending her around the tripod of his camera. It is as if he teaches her to swim. As if he teaches acrobatics. As if he could form her into something wet that he delivers out of one life into another.

And it is such a private thing the thing they do.

He is forming her into the wallpaper. He is smoothing her down into the flowers there. He is finding her nipples there. And he is kissing her pubis there.

He climbs into the wallpaper among the flowers. And his buttocks move in and out of the wall.

(1976)

to a dark moses

You are the one
I am lit for.

Come with your rod
that twists
and is a serpent.

I am the bush.
I am burning
I am not consumed.

(1974)

Heart Art

A man is masturbating his heart out,
Swinging in the hammock of the Internet.
He rocks back and forth, his cursor points
And selects. He swings between repetitive extremes
Among the come-ons in the chat rooms.
But finally he clicks on one
World Wide Web woman who cares.

Each of her virtual hairs
Brings him to his knees.
Each of her breasts
Projects like a sneeze.
He hears her dawning toward him as he reads her dimensions,
Waves sailing the seas of cyberspace—
Information, zeros-and-ones, whitecaps of.

Caught in a tangle of Internet,
Swinging in the mesh to sleep,
Rocking himself awake, sailing the virtual seas,
A man travels through space to someone inside
An active matrix screen. Snow falls.
A field of wildflowers blooms. Night falls.
Day resumes.

This is the story about humans taking over
The country. New York is outside
His study while he works. Paris is outside.
Outside the window is Bologna.
He logs on. He gets up.
He sits down. A car alarm goes off
Yoi yoi yoi yoi and yips as it suddenly stops.

Man has the takeover impact
Of an asteroid—throwing up debris, blotting out the sun—
Causing the sudden mass extinction
Of the small bookstore
At the millennium. The blood from the blast cakes
And forms the planet's new crust:
A hacker in Kinshasa getting it on with one in Nome.

Their poems start
With the part about masturbating the heart—
Saber cuts whacking a heart into tartare—
Heart art worldwide,
Meaning that even in the Far East the subject is love.
Here in the eastern United States,
A man is masturbating his art out.

An Ice Age that acts hot
Only because of the greenhouse effect
Is the sort of personality.
Beneath the dome of depleted ozone, they stay cold.
Mastodons are mating on the Internet
Over the bones of dinosaur nuclear arms,
Mating with their hands.

(1998)

MARGE PIERCY (BORN 1936)

Salt in the Afternoon

The room is a conch shell
and echoing in it, the blood
rushes in the ears,
the surf of desire sliding in
on the warm beach.

The room is the shell of the moon
snail, gorgeous predator
whose shell winds round and round
the color of moonshine
on your pumping back.

The bed is a slipper shell
on which we rock, opaline
and pearled with light sweat,
two great deep currents
colliding into white water.

The clam shell opens.
The oyster is eaten.
The squid shoots its white ink.
Now there is nothing but warm
salt puddles on the flats.

(1992)

C. K. WILLIAMS (BORN 1936)

∾

Ethics

The only time, I swear, I ever fell more than abstractly in love with some-
      one else's wife,
I managed to maintain the clearest sense of innocence, even after the
      woman returned my love,
even after she'd left her husband and come down on the plane from
      Montreal to be with me,
I still felt I'd done nothing immoral, that whole disturbing category had
      somehow been effaced;
even after she'd arrived and we'd gone home and gone to bed, and even
      after, the next morning,
when she crossed my room undressed—I almost looked away; we were
      both as shy as adolescents—
and all that next day when we walked, made love again, then slept, cling-
      ing to each other,
even then, her sleeping hand softly on my chest, her gentle breath gently
      moving on my cheek,
even then, or not until then, not until the new day touched upon us, and
      I knew, knew absolutely,
that though we might love each other, something in her had to have the
      husband, too,
and though she'd tried, and would keep trying to overcome herself, I
      couldn't wait for her,
did that perfect guiltlessness, that sure conviction of my inviolable virtue,
      flee me,
to leave me with a blade of loathing for myself, a disgust with who I
      guessed by now I was,
but even then, when I took her to the airport and she started up that cor-
      ridor the other way,
and we waved, just waved—anybody watching would have thought that
      we were separating friends—
even then, one part of my identity kept claiming its integrity, its non-
      involvement, even chastity,

which is what I castigate myself again for now, not the husband or his
      pain, which he survived,
nor the wife's temptation, but the thrill of evil that I'd felt, then kept
      myself from feeling.

(1992)

Breasts

I love breasts, hard
Full breasts, guarded
By a button.

They come in the night.
The bestiaries of the ancients
Which include the unicorn
Have kept them out.

Pearly, like the east
An hour before sunrise,
Two ovens of the only
Philosopher's stone
Worth bothering about.

They bring on their nipples
Beads of inaudible sighs,
Vowels of delicious clarity
For the little red schoolhouse of our mouths.

Elsewhere, solitude
Makes another gloomy entry
In its ledger, misery
Borrows another cup of rice.

They draw nearer: Animal
Presence. In the barn
The milk shivers in the pail.

I like to come up to them
From underneath, like a kid

Who climbs on a chair
To reach a jar of forbidden jam.

Gently, with my lips,
Loosen the button.
Have them slip into my hands
Like two freshly poured beer mugs.

I spit on fools who fail to include
Breasts in their metaphysics,
Star-gazers who have not enumerated them
Among the moons of the earth . . .

They give each finger
Its true shape, its joy:
Virgin soap, foam
On which our hands are cleansed.

And how the tongue honors
These two sour buns,
For the tongue is a feather
Dipped in egg-yolk.

I insist that a girl
Stripped to the waist
Is the first and last miracle,

That the old janitor on his deathbed
Who demands to see the breasts of his wife
For one last time
Is the greatest poet who ever lived.

O my sweet yes, my sweet no,
Look, everyone is asleep on the earth.

Now, in the absolute immobility
Of time, drawing the waist
Of the one I love to mine,

I will tip each breast
Like a dark heavy grape
Into the hive
Of my drowsy mouth.

(1974)

⁓

Pinup

The murkiness of the local garage is not so dense
that you cannot make out the calendar of pinup
drawings on the wall above a bench of tools.
Your ears are ringing with the sound of
the mechanic hammering on your exhaust pipe,
and as you look closer you notice that this month's
is not the one pushing the lawn mower, wearing
a straw hat and very short blue shorts,
her shirt tied in a knot just below her breasts.
Nor is it the one in the admiral's cap, bending
forward, resting her hands on a wharf piling,
glancing over the tiny anchors on her shoulders.
No, this is March, the month of great winds,
so appropriately it is the one walking her dog
along a city sidewalk on a very blustery day.
One hand is busy keeping her hat down on her head
and the other is grasping the little dog's leash,
so of course there is no hand left to push down
her dress which is billowing up around her waist
exposing her long stockinged legs and yes the secret
apparatus of her garter belt. Needless to say,
in the confusion of wind and excited dog
the leash has wrapped itself around her ankles
several times giving her a rather bridled
and helpless appearance which is added to
by the impossibly high heels she is teetering on.
You would like to come to her rescue,
gather up the little dog in your arms,
untangle the leash, lead her to safety,
and receive her bottomless gratitude, but
the mechanic is calling you over to look
at something under your car. It seems that he has
run into a problem and the job is going

to cost more than he had said and take
much longer than he had thought.
Well, it can't be helped, you hear yourself say
as you return to your place by the workbench,
knowing that as soon as the hammering resumes
you will slowly lift the bottom of the calendar
just enough to reveal a glimpse of what
the future holds in store: ah,
the red polka-dot umbrella of April and her
upturned palm extended coyly into the rain.

(1995)

ა

Desire

A woman in my class wrote that she is sick
of men wanting her body and when she reads
her poem out loud the other women all nod
and even some of the men lower their eyes

and look abashed as if ready to unscrew
their cocks and pound down their own dumb heads
with these innocent sausages of flesh, and none
would think of confessing his hunger

or admit how desire can ring like a constant
low note in the brain or grant how the sight
of a beautiful woman can make him groan
on those first spring days when the parkas

have been packed away and the bodies are staring
at the bodies and the eyes stare at the ground;
and there was a man I knew who even at ninety
swore that his desire had never diminished.

Is this simply the wish to procreate, the world
telling the cock to eat faster, while the cock
yearns for that moment when it forgets its loneliness
and the world flares up in an explosion of light?

Why have men been taught to feel ashamed
of their desire, as if each were a criminal
out on parole, a desperado with a long record
of muggings, rapes, such conduct as excludes

each one from all but the worst company,
and never to be trusted, no never to be trusted?

Why must men pretend to be indifferent as if each
were a happy eunuch engaged in spiritual thoughts?

But it's the glances that I like, the quick ones,
the unguarded ones, like a hand snatching a pie
from a window ledge and the feet pounding away;
eyes fastening on a leg, a breast, the curve

of a buttock, as the pulse takes an extra thunk
and the cock, that toothless worm, stirs in its sleep,
and fat possibility swaggers into the world
like a big spender entering a bar. And sometimes

the woman glances back. Oh, to disappear
in a tangle of fabric and flesh as the cock
sniffs out its little cave, and the body hungers
for closure, for the completion of the circle,

as if each of us were born only half a body
and we spend our lives searching for the rest.
What good does it do to deny desire, to chain
the cock to the leg and scrawl a black X

across its bald head, to hold out a hand
for each passing woman to slap? Better
to be bad and unrepentant, better to celebrate
each difference, not to be cruel or gluttonous

or overbearing, but full of hope and self-forgiving.
The flesh yearns to converse with other flesh.
Each pore loves to linger over its particular story.
Let these seconds not be full of self-recrimination

and apology. What is desire but the wish for some
relief from the self, the prisoner let out
into a small square of sunlight with a single
red flower and a bird crossing the sky, to lean back

against the bricks with the legs outstretched,
to feel the sun warming the brow, before returning

to one's mortal cage, steel doors slamming
in the cell block, steel bolts sliding shut?

(1991)

ROBERT HASS (BORN 1941)

Against Botticelli

1

In the life we lead together every paradise is lost.
Nothing could be easier: summer gathers new leaves
to casual darkness. So few things we need to know.
And the old wisdoms shudder in us and grow slack.
Like renunciation. Like the melancholy beauty
of giving it all up. Like walking steadfast
in the rhythms, winter light and summer dark.
And the time for cutting furrows and the dance.
Mad seed. Death waits it out. It waits us out,
the sleek incandescent saints, earthly and prayerful.
In our modesty. In our shamefast and steady attention
to the ceremony, its preparation, the formal hovering
of pleasure which falls like the rain we pray not to get
and are glad for and drown in. Or spray of that sea,
irised: otters in the tide lash, in the kelp-drench,
mammal warmth and the inhuman element. Ah, that is the secret.
That she is an otter, that Botticelli saw her so.
That we are not otters and are not in the painting
by Botticelli. We are not even in the painting by Bosch
where the people are standing around looking at the frame
of the Botticelli painting and when Love arrives, they throw up.
Or the Goya painting of the sad ones, angular and shriven,
who watch the Bosch and feel very compassionate
but hurt each other often and inefficiently. We are not in any painting.
If we do it at all, we will be like the old Russians.
We'll walk down through scrub oak to the sea
and where the seals lie preening on the beach
we will look at each other steadily
and butcher them and skin them.

2

The myth they chose was the constant lovers.
The theme was richness over time.
It is a difficult story and the wise never choose it
because it requires a long performance
and because there is nothing, by definition, between the acts.
It is different in kind from a man and the pale woman
he fucks in the ass underneath the stars
because it is summer and they are full of longing
and sick of birth. They burn coolly
like phosphorus, and the thing need be done
only once. Like the sacking of Troy
it survives in imagination,
in the longing brought perfectly to closing,
the woman's white hands opening, opening,
and the man churning inside her, thrashing there.
And light travels as if all the stars they were under
exploded centuries ago and they are resting now, glowing.
The woman thinks what she is feeling is like the dark
and utterly complete. The man is past sadness,
though his eyes are wet. He is learning about gratitude,
how final it is, as if the grace in Botticelli's *Primavera*,
the one with sad eyes who represents pleasure,
had a canvas to herself, entirely to herself.

(1979)

LINDA GREGG (BORN 1942)

Kept Burning and Distant

You return when you feel like it,
like rain. And like rain you are tender,
with the rain's inept tenderness.
A passion so general I could be anywhere.
You carry me out into the wet air.
You lay me down on the leaves
and the strong thing is not the sex
but waking up alone under trees after.

(1991)

SHARON OLDS (BORN 1942)

The Sisters of Sexual Treasure

As soon as my sister and I got out of our
mother's house, all we wanted to
do was fuck, obliterate
her tiny sparrow body and narrow
grasshopper legs. The men's bodies
were like our father's body! The massive
hocks, flanks, thighs, elegant
knees, long tapered calves—
we could have him there, the steep forbidden
buttocks, backs of the knees, the cock
in our mouth, ah the cock in our mouth.
                Like explorers who
discover a lost city, we went
nuts with joy, undressed the men
slowly and carefully, as if
uncovering buried artifacts that
proved our theory of the lost culture:
that if Mother said it wasn't there,
it was there.

(1978)

LOUISE GLÜCK (BORN 1943)

❦

The Encounter

You came to the side of the bed
and sat staring at me.
Then you kissed me—I felt
hot wax on my forehead.
I wanted it to leave a mark:
that's how I knew I loved you.
Because I wanted to be burned, stamped,
to have something in the end—
I drew the gown over my head;
a red flush covered my face and shoulders.
It will run its course, the course of fire,
setting a cold coin on the forehead, between the eyes.
You lay beside me; your hand moved over my face
as though you had felt it also—
you must have known, then, how I wanted you.
We will always know that, you and I.
The proof will be my body.

(1982)

SANDRA ALCOSSER (BORN 1944)

∾

By the Nape

Though sun rubbed honey slow
down rose hips, the world lost
its tenderness. Nipple-haired, joint-swollen,
the grasses waved for attention.
I wanted a watery demonstration for love,
more than wingpaper, twisted stalk of heartleaf.
Squalls rushed over pearling the world,
enlarging the smallest gesture, as I waited
for a drake in first winter plumage
to stretch his neck, utter a grunt whistle,
begin his ritualized display.
I'd held a wild mallard in my palm,
hoodlum heart whooping like a blood balloon.
I'd watched a woman suck coins
between her thighs and up inside her body.
How long she must have trained to let the cold world
enter so. The old man said his neighbor asked him
to milk her breasts, spray the walls, bathe in it.
That was his idea of paradise.
Sometimes I don't know who I am—
my age, my sex, my species—
only that I am an animal who will love
and die, and the soft plumage of another body
gives me pleasure, as I listen for the bubbling
and drumming, the exaggerated drinking
of a lover rising vertically from the sedges
to expose the violet streaks inside his body,
the vulnerable question of a nape.

(1998)

Resolution

Whereas the porch screen sags from
The weight of flowers (impatiens) that grew
Against it, then piles of wet leaves,
Then drifted snow; and

Whereas, now rolled like absence in its
Drooping length, a dim gold wave,
Sundown's last, cast across a sea of clouds
And the floating year, almost reaches
The legs of the low-slung chair; and

Whereas between bent trees flies
And bees twirl above apples
And peaches fallen on blue gravel; and

Whereas yesterday's thunder shook blossoms
Off laurel the day after they appeared; and

Whereas in the dust, the fine and perfect
Dust of cat-paw prints scattered across
The gleaming car hood, something
Softer than blossoms falls away,
Something your lips left on mine; and

Whereas it's anyone's guess as to how long
It's been since a humid day sank so low,
So far from the present that missing
Sensations or the sensation of something
Missing have left impressions in the air,
The kind a head leaves on a pillow; and

Whereas the last of ancient, unconvincing
Notions evaporate from the damp pages

Of thick, old books that describe how,
For instance, Time and Love once
Lay together here; how in a slurred flash
Of light she turned and waded back
Into the sea, and how the slack
Part of any day was and is
All in the way he, half
Asleep, felt her hand slip out of his; and

Whereas, the blue heron stands on the shore;
While the sleek heron turns, broad
To narrow, half hidden among the reeds;
Turning with the stealth, the sweep
Of twilight's narrowing minute,
Of stillness taking aim; turning
Until it almost disappears into
The arrowhead instant the day disappears,
Until staring out of the reeds,
The aforementioned heron
Is more felt than seen; and

Whereas, you, with due forethought
And deliberation, bite into
An apple's heart and wish it were your own

(1999)

133

ROBERT OLEN BUTLER (BORN 1945)

◌

Walter Raleigh, courtier and explorer, beheaded by King James I, 1618

Bess my dear old queen my Elizabeth her lips brittle her body
smelling sharply beneath the clove and cinnamon from her
pomander she lies next to me in the dark still besmocked
though the night is warm and she has asked me here at last
and I am masted for her and her bedchamber is black as
pitch so she is but a shadow *no torch* she cried as I entered
upon pain of death and now we are arranged thus my own
nakedness perhaps too quick she says *call your new-found
land the place of the virgin, Virginia, to honor my lifelong
state* and I flinch but her smock does rise and I find the
mouth of her Amazon her long fingers scrawling upon my
back a history of the world *oh sir oh sir you have found the
city of gold at last* she says, knowing me well this fills my
sails the jungles of ancient lands are mine my queen *oh
swisser swatter* she cries and falls away and I lie beside her
staring into the dark, and I am sated certainly, but the
moment calls for some new thing, and I say *wait, my queen*
and I am out her door to the nearest torch and I have
already prepared the treasure from my new world, this
sweet sotweed this tobacco, and I sail back and slip in beside
her and we sit and we smoke

(2006)

∾

A Man and a Woman

Between a man and a woman
The anger is greater, for each man would like to sleep
In the arms of each woman who would like to sleep
In the arms of each man, if she trusted him not to be
Schizophrenic, if he trusted her not to be
A hypochondriac, if she trusted him not to leave her
Too soon, if he trusted her not to hold him
Too long, and often women stare at the word men
As it lives in the word women, as if each woman
Carried a man inside her and a woe, and has
Crying fits that last for days, not like the crying
Of a man, which lasts a few seconds, and rips the throat
Like a claw—but because the pain differs
Much as the shape of the body, the woman takes
The suffering of the man for selfishness, the man
The woman's pain for helplessness, the woman's lack of it
For hardness, the man's tenderness for deception,
The woman's lack of acceptance, an act of contempt
Which is really fear, the man's fear for fickleness,
Yet cars come off the bridge in rivers of light
Each holding a man and a woman.

(1970)

BERNADETTE MAYER (BORN 1945)

First turn to me . . .

First turn to me after a shower,
you come inside me sideways as always

in the morning you ask me to be on top of you,
then we take a nap, we're late for school

you arrive at night inspired and drunk,
there is no reason for our clothes

we take a bath and lie down facing each other,
then later we turn over, finally you come

we face each other and talk about childhood
as soon as I touch your penis I wind up coming

you stop by in the morning to say hello
we sit on the bed indian fashion not touching

in the middle of the night you come home
from a nightclub, we don't get past the bureau

next day it's the table, and after that the chair
because I want so much to sit you down & suck your cock

you ask me to hold your wrists, but then when I
touch your neck with both my hands you come

it's early morning and you decide to very quietly
come on my knee because of the children

you've been away at school for centuries, your girlfriend
has left you, you come four times before morning

you tell me you masturbated in the hotel before you came by
I don't believe it, I serve the lentil soup naked

I massage your feet to seduce you, you are reluctant,
my feet wind up at your neck and ankles

you try not to come too quickly
also, you don't want to have a baby

I stand up from the bath, you say turn around
and kiss the backs of my legs and my ass

you suck my cunt for a thousand years, you are weary
at last I remember my father's anger and I come

you have no patience and come right away
I get revenge and won't let you sleep all night

we make out for so long we can't remember how
we wound up hitting our heads against the wall

I lie on my stomach, you put one hand under me
and one hand over me and that way can love me

you appear without notice and with flowers
I fall for it and we become missionaries

you say you can only fuck me up the ass when you are drunk
so we try it sober in a room at the farm

we lie together one night, exhausted couplets
and don't make love. does this mean we've had enough?

watching t.v. we wonder if each other wants to
interrupt the plot; later I beg you to read to me

like the Chinese we count 81 thrusts
then 9 more out loud till we both come

I come three times before you do
and then it seems you're mad and never will

it's only fair for a woman to come more
think of all the times they didn't care

(1992)

∽

Disparu

I spent the day with invisible you, your arms
invisible around me, holding me blue in your
open invisible eyes. We walked invisible,
invisible and happy, daydreaming sight as if
light were a piano it played on. Invisible
my hand at your well-cut trouser, invisible
speeding night, the invisible taxi, bare
the invisible legs, kissing the vanishing
mouths, breasts invisible, your, my invisible
entwining, the sheets white as geese, blue as sky.
And darling, how your invisible prick rose,
rosy, invisible, invisible as all night
galloping, swinging, we tilted and sang.

(2005)

STAR BLACK (BORN 1946)

The Evangelist

The devil is rising inside you, rising, rising, rising.
He is going to make you do something true, something
sinister and surprising, something demonic and inviting.
The devil is doing his work through you. He isn't hiding.

You are to burn in the gates of hell: trillions of years,
millenniums, millenniums. Angels are going to mourn for you
in their white, white dresses. Harps will plink sad songs:
you're the one Peter erases: wrong, wrong, very wrong.

The devil is on your back, riding. The devil is on your back,
gliding. The devil is on your back, whispering words, words
that are heard: sinful, succulent, lascivious words, horror
sounds, coming, coming, rising through you, pitchforked

thumping, hurrying, your veins tubes, hurrying, thunder
ooze, tromp, tromp, tromp, the devil is taking you.

(2007)

ELLEN BASS (BORN 1947)

∾

Gate C22

At gate C22 in the Portland airport
a man in a broad-band leather hat kissed
a woman arriving from Orange County.
They kissed and kissed and kissed. Long after
the other passengers clicked the handles of their carry-ons
and wheeled briskly toward short-term parking,
the couple stood there, arms wrapped around each other
like he'd just staggered off the boat at Ellis Island,
like she'd been released at last from ICU, snapped
out of a coma, survived bone cancer, made it down
from Annapurna in only the clothes she was wearing.

Neither of them was young. His beard was gray.
She carried a few extra pounds you could imagine
her saying she had to lose. But they kissed lavish
kisses like the ocean in the early morning,
the way it gathers and swells, sucking
each rock under, swallowing it
again and again. We were all watching —
passengers waiting for the delayed flight
to San Jose, the stewardesses, the pilots,
the aproned woman icing Cinnabons, the man selling
sunglasses. We couldn't look away. We could
taste the kisses crushed in our mouths.

But the best part was his face. When he drew back
and looked at her, his smile soft with wonder, almost
as though he were a mother still open from giving birth,
as your mother must have looked at you, no matter
what happened after — if she beat you or left you or
you're lonely now — you once lay there, the vernix
not yet wiped off, and someone gazed at you
as if you were the first sunrise seen from the earth.

The whole wing of the airport hushed,
all of us trying to slip into that woman's middle-aged body,
her plaid Bermuda shorts, sleeveless blouse, glasses,
little gold hoop earrings, tilting our heads up.

(2002)

AI (BORN 1947)

Twenty-Year Marriage

You keep me waiting in a truck
with its one good wheel stuck in the ditch,
while you piss against the south side of a tree.
Hurry. I've got nothing on under my skirt tonight.
That still excites you, but this pickup has no windows
and the seat, one fake leather thigh,
pressed close to mine is cold.
I'm the same size, shape, make as twenty years ago,
but get inside me, start the engine;
you'll have the strength, the will to move.
I'll pull, you push, we'll tear each other in half.
Come on, baby, lay me down on my back.
Pretend you don't owe me a thing
and maybe we'll roll out of here,
leaving the past stacked up behind us;
old newspapers nobody's ever got to read again.

(1973)

143

JANE KENYON (1947–1995)

The Shirt

The shirt touches his neck
and smoothes over his back.
It slides down his sides.
It even goes down below his belt—
down into his pants.
Lucky shirt.

(1978)

Lust

If only he could touch her,
Her name like an old wish
In the stopped weather of salt
On a snail. He longs to be

Words, juicy as passionfruit
On her tongue. He'd do anything,
Would dance three days & nights
To make the most terrible gods

Rise out of ashes of the yew,
To step from the naked
Fray, to be as tender
As meat imagined off

The bluegill's pearlish
Bones. He longs to be
An orange, to feel fingernails
Run a seam through him.

(2000)

145

She Lays

She lays each beautifully mooned finger
in the furrow on the right and on the left
sides of her clitoris and lets them linger
in their swollen cribs until the wish to see the shaft
exposed lets her move her fingers at the same time
to the right and to the left sides pinning back
the labia in a nest of hair, the pink sack
of folds exposed, the purplish ridge she'll climb
when she lets one hand re-pin the labia
to free the other to wander with a withheld
purpose as if it were lost in the sands when the Via
To The City suddenly appeared, *exposed:*
when the whole exhausted mons is finally held by
both hands is when the Via gates are closed,

but they are open now, as open as her
thighs lying open among the arranged pillows.
Secrets have no place in the orchid boat of her
body and old pink brain beneath the willows.
This is self-love, assured, and this is lost time.
This is knowing, knowing, known
since growing, growing, grown;
revelation without astonishment,
understanding what is meant.
This is world-love. This is lost I'm.

(1984)

∾

The Body Is the Flower

So bondage is a big part of it, after all—
that old art of rendering a lover submissive:
a tactic, a strategy. Denying somebody's body
the power to move denies that body the power
to be believed. Isn't that what's so sexual?
The intimate plea? The fear you can't go back?

Until your lover throws you over on your back.
Maybe a woman becomes a man, then. After all,
it's the head games that conjure up the sexual:
which one agrees, this time, to be submissive;
which one straps on the fetishes, the powers,
we make to make the body yield up the body . . .

O the rendering, the surrendering of the body!
We so much want to go back, all the way back . . .
You stand before a mirror, naked, the power
of someone's eyes, words, erasing you, the all
you claim to be. Belief can be so submissive:
desire, not truth. But being believed is sexual

vantage: the crying out, the echo, the sexual
need you never knew could subjugate the body . . .
So you cry out at the idea of her, submissive,
yes, her hands your hands, *yes,* leading you back,
her voice your voice, *o god,* eyes lips cunt all
mirroring, *yes,* the glory, *o god yes,* the power . . .

Later, you wipe off the remnants of the power
with Kleenex. When you get down to the sexual
level, you get sexually levelled, that's all:
doesn't discipline make a believer of the body?

You whisper no name but hers in the going back.
Tomorrow, it will be her turn to be submissive:

the ties that bind render you both submissive.
You'll need her to believe your plea, her power;
she'll need you to escort her all the way back,
before the life alongside this life, her body
alongside yours: ravenous, indifferent, sexual.
There, anything might happen, anything at all,

if all you need is to be believed. The power
of the sexual plea masquerades as the submissive
act. The body is the flower of the going back.

(1994)

HEATHER McHUGH (BORN 1948)

∾

Gig at Big Al's

There is a special privacy onstage.
Wearing little, then less, then
nudity's silver high-
heeled shoes, I dance to myself: the men

posed below at tables
with assessors' gazes and the paycheck's
sure prerogatives are dreams
I've realized, my chosen

people, made-up eyes, my fantasies.
I pull down dark around the room.
I turn on sex's juke two-step.
I set foot on the spotlight's

isolated space and grease
my hips and lick my legs. With a whip
lash of gin in the first row anyone
can beat around the bush, can buy

my brand of loneliness, all possible
circumlocutions of crotch. No one
can touch me, by law
I cannot touch myself. So none

of it is public, not until
in one side door
on his soft shoes
my lover comes to watch.

(1977)

LYNN EMANUEL (BORN 1949)

❧

Dreaming of Rio at Sixteen

It was always Raoul's kisses or grandmother's
diamond earrings that burned like Brazilian noons
while you and she sheeted beds finding every
beautiful mother an excuse to stop and look
as they moved in sling-back shoes past Lloyd's
Esso then into the movies' cool arcades.

Taking off your clothes, sometimes sixteen was
that, sometimes it was not naked but wore
a collar at its throat and gloves, kissed
with its mouth closed, over and over, like the pinch
of a tight shoe. Even all buttoned up, sixteen
was semitropic and summer had put out every lure:

a whole plantation of perfect grasses.
Lynnskala, Lynnksala your grandmother called,
her voice grinding uphill, heavier and heavier,
with its load of anger. Old stab in the dark
stood on the back porch stirring her spoon around
in the dinner bell and calling you in the voice that now

held its hands across its heart, *Come home, come
home save yourself for a wedding,* while you,
beside the Amazon, were all teeth, all boat.

(1992)

Poem

Loving you is every bit as fine
as coming over a hill into the sun
at ninety miles an hour darling when
it's dawn and you can hear the stars unlocking
themselves from the designs of God beneath
the disintegrating orchestra of my black
Chevrolet. The radio clings to an un-
identified station—somewhere a tango suffers,
and the dance floor burns around two lovers
whom nothing can touch—no, not even death!
Oh! the acceleration with which my heart does proceed,
reaching like stars almost but never quite
of light the speed of light the speed of light.

(1987)

DANA GIOIA (BORN 1950)

❧

Alley Cat Love Song

Come into the garden, Fred,
For the neighborhood tabby is gone.
Come into the garden, Fred.
I have nothing but my flea collar on,
And the scent of catnip has gone to my head.
I'll wait by the screen door till dawn.

The fireflies court in the sweetgum tree.
The nightjar calls from the pine,
And she seems to say in her rhapsody,
"Oh, mustard-brown Fred, be mine!"
The full moon lights my whiskers afire,
And the fur goes erect on my spine.

I hear the frogs in the muddy lake
Croaking from shore to shore.
They've one swift season to soothe their ache.
In autumn they sing no more.
So ignore me now, and you'll hear my meow
As I scratch all night at the door.

(2001)

PAUL JONES (BORN 1950)

⁓

To His Penis

after the medieval Welsh poem "Cywydd y Gal,"
by Dafydd ap Gwilym

By God, Penis, gypsy gland,
you'll be guarded with eye and hand.
You stand convicted, straight-headed pole,
of all crass crimes possible;
cunt's quill, I'll bridle your snout,
rein you in, lest you creep out.
Take this warning, stiff stinger:
No jamming with jealous singers.

Wretched rolling pin, scrotum's crown,
don't rise up, don't wave around!
God's gift to good church ladies,
column for their cavities,
sweet snare trigger, sleek young swan
asleep in his own soft down,
moist gun, slick milk-giving switch,
fresh-grown sprout. Be still! Don't twitch!
Crooked and blunt, accursed spindle,
spike where prim pussies impale;
eel's harsh head, hearty and brave,
abrupt bar, bundle of staves.
You swell thicker than men's thighs;
drill that never dulls, love's spy,
auger who drives deep below,
leather veined lavender-blue,
scepter that grants lusts to grow,
bolt that seals women's arses closed.

The hole in your top, like a pipe,
whistles "fuck" when luck is ripe.

Your strange sight makes all women
charming and comely and warm;
round grinder, hound on the hunt,
you light fire to young tight cunts;
roof-beam boosting maiden's laps,
your prod sets all bells to clap;
brash rod, you've tilled twenty rows,
groin growth raised like a grand nose,
crude inconstant crotch crawler,
lanky and lewd loving lure,
gnarled yet graceful, a goose neck.
Hard nail, you left my home wrecked.

You're arrested; reed-tall thruster;
hang your head low; loin lounger,
you've come under my control,
bold witch's wand; woe to your soul.
Why am I scorned and called "bad"
when wicked wisdom wins your head?

(1999)

The Snake in the Garden Considers Daphne

My less erotic god condemned
my taste for girls less classical
than you, the kind that can't resist
a dazzling advance or trees that stand
for love. Of course I understand
up there it seems to be all light
and prelapsarian elation—but bear
in mind your lower half that gropes
for water, the slender roots you spread
in secret to fascinate the rocks,
while sunlight pries apart your leaves
and flights of birds arouse the air
around you. If only I could run
a brazen hand along this wood
and feel your heart accelerate
beneath it, rising to your lips.
If only you could pick the whitest
petals from the holy orchard
where I patrol the crevices
and slink along my damned gut,
you could arrange them as you wished
and change the ending of our story.
But we're disarmed, and nothing changes
in our natural gardens—we cannot grasp
the word *hope*, which the ones we've tempted
find always at their fingertips.

(1994)

It Never Happened

She licked an invisible command from his palm—
He looked forward to the old days to come.

She let the hot wax trickle down his chest—
He recalled the harshness of certain ruins.

She smiled and asked: "Do you like my breasts?"—
He realized courage doesn't last very long.

—There was a bright glade of rose and fern.
—The moon was rising; iron shadows fell.

She said: "This isn't appropriate," then cooed like a bird—
It was the sweetest, most seductive sound he ever heard.

Afterward, she said: "It never happened, so don't write about it."
He sang a silent hymn to the blank pages floating down the river.

She said: "I am the enemy of your destiny."—
He said: "I am the heat-sink memory that absorbs your frenzy."

Thunder and lightning struck again.
Soon after, the mattress caught fire,

And was thrown out the window onto Washington Street.
In her mind, snakes replaced the birds that had supplanted the fish.

He read her mind; his hair was singed; he said: "Fuck evolution."
She moaned: "Oh yes—oh my God, *please* fuck evolution."

(2007)

JUDITH HALL (BORN 1951)

❧

In an Empty Garden

Better to fall, better to fall than wait
To be held in air; wanting to be held,
Held in words we use when we embrace.
I wanted to be held in air or fall,

To be held in air. Wanting to be held,
I fell along the air's slow drawl,
Wanting to be held in air or fall,
As the turning, of a body turned a voice away.

I fell along the air's slow drawl,
Away from words *abundance, blame,*
As he turned his body, turned his voice away,
As if I shed the words and gave them shape.

The word *abundance,* the word *blame:*
I handed him a place to put his tongue
And shed the words and gave them shape:
A snake, turning his skin into a skeleton.

I handed him a place to put his tongue,
A place where we knew why we kissed.
Like a snake, turning his skin into a skeleton,
I turned the air to kisses, golden nipples,

Any place. I knew why we kissed.
Another apple, another, another tongue.
The air will turn to kisses, golden nipples.
He wanted me to say I did it: Touched

Another apple, another, another tongue.
I will not tell you what we whispered.

He wanted me to say I did it, touched
A history of wishes to be held.

I will not tell you what we whispered.
I wanted him to help me question
A history of wishes: to be held,
Waiting, again, for that first kiss.

Help me. Help me question
The words we use when we embrace,
Waiting again for that first kiss—
Better to fall, better to fall than wait.

(1992)

CYNTHIA HUNTINGTON (BORN 1951)

∿

From *Shot Up in the Sexual Revolution*
(The True Adventures of Suzy Creamcheese)

So, I slept with my lovers, I slept with my friends,
my lovers' friends and my friends' lovers,
friends of friends and so on. I slept with my dealer
and my dealer's dealer, just to be sure.
I slept with some men I barely knew
to prove I was open-minded, or to avoid an argument,
and I slept with some men I didn't like
just to be nice, or, well, to avoid an argument.
You might say I had an open-door policy.

I took it three ways, I took it sideways:
"thousands of men and a few hundred women."
Hum jobs, tie me up, half-and-half, and fuck the dog.
I took it in the ass, in my mouth, between my thighs
and way up inside from any angle. Yet what I loved most
was hard dancing to loud music: that beat through the floor,
and bodies swaying, sweating, the tension building,
and getting just to the edge of it, in a room, in a woods,
down a hallway wedged inside a bathroom stall, falling
down fast, or leaning back brace yourself
on the wall, diving into it like stepping on a mine—just
blowing yourself up, all the while holding on
to some sweating panting guy also blowing himself up—
just kick out the door hard mindless sex—I wanted it
as much as the next guy, the next high priestess of come,
and it was ours and all new and fine, and would never end,

until one day love comes roiling up like swamp gas
fermented for years in the collective unconscious
of old songs and bad movies, a distant memory wakening.
His thumbs in his belt loops, his crooked smile

and dark moods, and you think this one is a god
or an avatar of destiny, and you're nothing unless
he loves you too, and now everything is changed
and you let your life go, like a bad gene or a slow virus.
You've bought the gypsy's curse, the heroine's undoing,
that fatal weakness inscribed in a hundred novels
you read as a girl in your sweet gabled bedroom
while you were waiting for your life to happen.

(2005)

∾

The Little Black Book

It was Aisling who first soft-talked my penis tip between
      her legs
while teasing open that Velcro strip between her legs.

Cliona then. A skinny country girl.
The small stream, in which I would skinny-dip, between
      her legs.

Born and bred in Londinium, the standoffish Etain,
who kept a stiff upper lip between her legs.

Grainne. Grain goddess. The last, triangular shock of corn,
through which a sickle might rip, between her legs.

Again and again that winter I made a beeline for Ita,
for the sugar-water sip between her legs.

The spring brought not only Liadan but her memory of
      Cuirithir,
his ghostly one-upmanship between her legs.

(Ita is not to be confused with her steely half sister,
      Niamh,
she of the ferruginous drip between her legs.)

It was Niamh, as luck would have it, who introduced me
      to Orla.
The lost weekend of a day trip between *her* legs.

It was Orla, as luck would have it, who introduced me to
      Roisin.
The bramble patch. The rosehip between her legs.

What ever became of Sile?
Sile, who led me to horse-worship between her legs.

As for Janet from the Shankill, who sometimes went by
    "Sinead,"
I practiced my double back flip between her legs.

I had a one-on-one tutorial with Siobhan.
I read *The Singapore Grip* between her legs.

And what ever became of Sorcha, Sorcha, Sorcha?
Her weakness for the whip between her legs.

Or the big-boned, broad-shouldered Treasa?
She asked me to give her a buzz clip between her legs.

Or the little black sheep, Una, who kept her own little
    black book?
I fluttered, like an erratum slip, between her legs.

(1998)

From *Slave Sonnets*

I've been a shit and I hate fucking you now
because I love fucking you too much;
what good's the head of my cock inside you
when my other head, the one with the brains,
keeps thinking how fucked up everything is,
how fucked I am to be fucking you and thinking
these things which take me away from you
when all I want is to be close to you
but fuck you for letting me fuck you now
when all that connects us is this fucking cock
which is as lost inside you as I am, here,
in the dark, fucking you and thinking—fuck,
the wallpaper behind you had a name,
what was it? You called it what? Herringbone?

(1986)

∾

The Shipfitter's Wife

I loved him most
when he came home from work,
his fingers still curled from fitting pipe,
his denim shirt ringed with sweat
and smelling of salt, the drying weeds
of the ocean. I would go to him where he sat
on the edge of the bed, his forehead
anointed with grease, his cracked hands
jammed between his thighs, and unlace
the steel-toed boots, stroke his ankles,
his calves, the pads and bones of his feet.
Then I'd open his clothes and take
the whole day inside me—the ship's
gray sides, the miles of copper pipe,
the voice of the first man clanging
off the hull's silver ribs, spark of lead
kissing metal, the clamp, the winch,
the white fire of the torch, the whistle
and the long drive home.

(1998)

PETER SERCHUK (BORN 1952)

∽

The Naked Women

Just when I thought the world
was racing to its end I see them
everywhere; ordering lattes at
Starbucks, bent over crocuses
and daffodils, waiting for buses
and taxis in earrings and heels while
morning finger-paints their backs.

On the streets joggers illuminate
the mundane. At the bank, the same
long line now seems like courtesy
thanks to the teller in Window 2.
And I marvel at the hand of justice
when a policewoman tickets
my car wearing only a pen.

What a wild world we live in,
puppets of money and fear,
as if this brief stop in Eden was
little more than a business trip.
While neighbors hoard tax cuts
and prepare for the apocalypse,
I'm comforted by the evening news;

tan lines cupping the implants of
the anchorwoman who referees
Muslims and Jews, zealots chasing
the innocent with prayer books
and guns while the meteorologist
brings a warming front to my
free and private continent.

(2006)

DENNIS COOPER (BORN 1953)

After School, Street Football,
Eighth Grade

Their jeans sparkled, cut off
way above the knee, and my
friends and I would watch them
from my porch, books of poems
lost in our laps, eyes wide as
tropical fish behind our glasses.

Their football flashed from hand
to hand, tennis shoes gripped
the asphalt, sweat's spotlight on
their strong backs. We would
dream of hugging them, and crouch
later in weird rooms, and come.

Once their ball fell our way
so two of them came over, hands
on their hips, asking us to
throw it to them, which Arthur did,
badly, and they chased it back.
One turned to yell, "Thanks"

and we dreamed of his long
teeth in our necks. We
wanted them to wander over,
place deep wet underarms to
our lips, and then their white
asses, then those loud mouths.

One day one guy was very tired,
didn't move fast enough,
so a car hit him and he sprawled

fifty feet away, sexy, but he was
dead, blood like lipstick, then
those great boys stood together

on the sidewalk and we joined them,
mixing in like one big friendship
to the cops, who asked if we were,
and those boys were too sad to counter.
We'd known his name, Tim, and how
he'd turned to thank us nicely

but now he was under a sheet
anonymous as God, the big boys crying,
spitting words, and we stunned
like intellectuals get, our high
voices soft as the tinkling of a
chandelier on a ceiling too high to see.

(1995)

Lilacs in NYC

Monday evening, E. 22nd
   in front of Jimmy and Vincent's,
a leafing maple, and it's as if

Manhattan existed in order
   to point to these
leaves, the urbane marvel

of them. Tuesday AM
   at the Korean market,
cut, bundled lilacs, in clear

or silvered cellophane—
   mist & inebriation,
cyclonic flames in tubs

of galvanized aluminum,
   all along Third Avenue,
as if from the hardy rootstocks

of these shops sprouted
   every leaf-shine and shade
of panicle: smoke, plum, lavender

like the sky over the Hudson,
   some spring evenings, held
in that intoxicating window

the horizontal avenues provide.
   Numbered avenues,
dumb beautiful ministers. . . . Later,

a whole row of white crabapples
   shivering in the wind
of a passing train; later,

a magnolia flaring
   in a scatter
of its own fallen petals,

towering out of a field
   of itself. Is that what
we do? I've felt like that,

straddling my lover,
   as if I rose
out of something

which resembled me,
   joined at the trunk
as if I come flaming

up out of what I am,
   the live foam muscling
beneath me. . . .

Strong bole thrust up
   into the billow,
into the frills and the insistences

and elaborations,
   the self flying open!
They're flowers, they know

to fall if they bloom;
   blessed relief of it,
not just myself this little while.

You enter me and we are strangers
   to ourselves but not
to each other, I enter you

(strange verb but what else
   to call it—to penetrate
to fuck to be inside of

none of the accounts of the body
   were ever really useful were they
tell the truth none of them),

I enter you (strange verb,
   as if we were each an enclosure
a shelter, imagine actually

considering yourself a *temple*)
   and violet the crush of shadows
that warm wrist that deep-hollowed

collar socket those salt-lustered
   lilacy shoulderblades,
in all odd shadings of green and dusk . . .

blooming in the field
   of our shatter. You enter me
and it's Macy's,

some available version of infinity;
   I enter you and I'm the grass,
covered with your shock

of petals out of which you rise
   Mr. April Mr. Splendor
climbing up with me

inside this rocking, lilac boat.
   My candlelight master,
who trembles me into smoke-violet,

as April does to lilac-wood.

(1998)

TONY HOAGLAND (BORN 1953)

∿

Visitation

Now when I visit Ellen's body in my memory,
it is like visiting a cemetery. I look
at the chiseled, muscular belly
and at the perfect thirty-year-old breasts
and the fine blond purse of her pussy
and I kneel and weep a little there.
I am not the first person to locate god
in erectile tissue and the lubricating gland
but when I kiss her breast and feel
the tough button of her nipple
rise and stiffen to my tongue
like the dome of a small mosque
in an ancient, politically incorrect city,
I feel holy, I begin to understand religion.
I circle around to see the basilica
of her high Irish-American butt,
and I look at her demure little asshole
and am sorry I didn't spend more time with it.
And her mouth and her eyes and white white teeth.
It's beauty beauty beauty which in a way Ellen
herself the person distracted me from. It's
beauty which has been redistributed now
by the justice of chance and the temporal economy.
Now I'm like a sad astronaut living
deep in space, breathing the oxygen of memory
out of a silver can. Now I'm like an angel
drifting over the surface of the earth,
brushing its meadows and forests
with the tips of my wings,
with wonder and regret and affection.

(2007)

RICHARD JONES (BORN 1953)

❧

Wan Chu's Wife in Bed

Wan Chu, my adoring husband,
has returned from another trip
selling trinkets in the provinces.
He pulls off his lavender shirt
as I lie naked in our bed,
waiting for him. He tells me
I am the only woman he'll ever love.
He may wander from one side of China
to the other, but his heart
will always stay with me.
His face glows in the lamplight
with the sincerity of a boy
when I lower the satin sheet
to let him see my breasts.
Outside, it begins to rain
on the cherry trees
he planted with our son,
and when he enters me with a sigh,
the storm begins in earnest,
shaking our little house.
Afterwards, I stroke his back
until he falls asleep.
I'd love to stay awake all night
listening to the rain,
but I should sleep, too.
Tomorrow Wan Chu will be
a hundred miles away
and I will be awake all night
in the arms of Wang Chen,
the tailor from Ming Pao,
the tiny village down the river.

(1996)

Pretty Piece of Tail

Pretty piece of tail,
now I wanted you so bad.
Nice, pretty piece of tail
and I wanted it mighty bad.
I thought if I could get it,
that piece be the best I ever had.

She had her legs together
the way her mama said she should.
Yeah, she was keeping her legs together
just like her mama say she should.
The way she was holding on to it,
I knew it must be good.

I schemed and lied to get it,
told her I loved her best.
That's right, I schemed and I lied to get it,
told the girl I loved her best.
Soon as I tried that little bit of tail,
I knew it was no better than the rest.

When I first saw you, baby,
I told you I'd love you until I die.
First time I saw you, looking so good now, baby,
said I'd love you till I die.
Well now I'll tell you, if you didn't know, darling,
a man's just born to lie.

That's the truth, I'll testify.

If I was on the jury,
talking about courts and jail—

If I was on the jury
wouldn't no man go to jail
just for trying out a pretty piece of tail.

(1982)

KIM ADDONIZIO (BORN 1954)

The Divorcée and Gin

I love the frosted pints you come in,
and the tall bottles with their uniformed men;
the bars where you're poured chilled
into shallow glasses, the taste of drowned olives,
and the scrawled benches where I see you
passed impatiently from one mouth
to another, the bag twisted tight around
your neck, the hand that holds you
shaking a little from its need
which is the true source of desire; God, I love
what you do to me at night when we're alone,
how you wait for me to take you into me
until I'm so confused with you I can't
stand up anymore. I know you want me
helpless, each cell whimpering, and I give
you that, letting you have me just the way
you like it. And when you're finished
you turn your face to the wall while I curl
around you again, and enter another morning
with aspirin and the useless ache
that comes from loving, too well,
those who, under the guise of pleasure,
destroy everything they touch.

(1995)

Mirrors

A while later that night they flurried in;
some were humming and laughing nervously.
"Have you assessed the deep indecency

most of you tend to feel at having sex
before the spread of a mirror? As though
another couple were in the room and

couldn't help peering at your pleasure or
peeking in your eyes? Who wouldn't flush red
at the sight of two bodies moving in

rhythm both with each other and with you?"
"But under that blush lies a deeper one—
the subliminal, sublunary sense

of being observed from another sphere."
"Thus the preference for modest mirrors,
hung well above the scene and frame of love,

which enhance the room's depth, yes, but offer
at best an oblique view to a watcher
at a higher vantage." "And note that those

who get a thrill from curling and rolling
before mirrors are voyeurs or else want
to be seen by voyeurs, which amounts to

the same thing: a racy view of others'
raptures or lascivious exposure
of one's own." Now the rills of laughter lulled:

"Despite our pleasure at reacquaintance
with breasts, balls, and lips, it is considered
in cosmic bad taste to show too much sex

to the other side." Is it (I was moved
to ask) nostalgic, tender, even raw
to look in later from a place apart?

Giving a low sigh, one spun and then spoke:
"The convocation of qualms and kisses,
the regrets, the assembly of regrets

for those not loved, for those not loved enough,
and for those who should never have been touched
—what else in this death could be more poignant?—

nothing being left of what might have been
but a half glance through a glaze of silver . . ."
And here one stopped. No, one could not go on.

(2000)

177

DEAN YOUNG (BORN 1955)

Platypus

Your pink cowboy hat is my vagina.
I wouldn't say that to just anyone.
When I see you in your buckeroo pj's,
I want to watch your face contort
like bacon as it fries
while my penis splits you into a holy star.
An orgasm is a spaceship.
You wait for many many years
then you are mature enough to have a mouse.
You practice putting immense feeling
into the tiny pelt.
The rest of your life you explode.

(2007)

AMY GERSTLER (BORN 1956)

❧

Ode to Semen

Whitish brine, spooners' gruel,
mortality's nectar, potent drool,
foam on oceans
where our ancestors first
bubbled up (that vast soup
we'll one day
be stirred back into). . . .
O gluey sequel
to kisses and licks,
the loins' shy outcry,
blurt of melted pearl
leaked into hungry mouths
or between splayed legs
in a dim, curtained room,
while far off, down the hall,
in the kitchen's overlit,
crumb-littered domain,
ham is sliced,
potatoes are peeled,
and, emitting pungent milk,
minced onions
begin to sizzle . . .

(2004)

SARAH MACLAY (BORN 1956)

❧

My Lavenderdom

—as in, pre-flutter, that kingdom of semi-purpleness—should I
    say *dome of*—that area of anti-limp, lawnless, drunk on your
    fingering, unfingering—that omnivore, oh, eating now your—
    even your branches, iceless, antifrozen, gazelle flying toward the
    twin kingdoms of your cheekness (more at "flying buttress"),
    nearly periwinkling now—that perpetrator of the semi-grunt,
    grunt, instigator of the groanful demi-flood of—flutter, flutter,
    post-flutter—gorge of neomauve, rich canal of sunsetish plush,
    now unguardedly sub-fuschia; that private brandied eyelash
    batting at you in its brashest postcool queenness, plump and
    succulent as a plum—

(2000)

Bareback Pantoum

One night, bareback and young, we rode through the woods
and the woods were on fire—
two borrowed horses, two local boys
whose waists we clung to, my sister and I,

and the woods were on fire—
the pounding of hooves and the smell of smoke and the sharp
    sweat of boys
whose waists we clung to, my sister and I,
as we rode toward flame with the sky in our mouths—

the pounding of hooves and the smell of smoke and the sharp
    sweat of boys
and the heart saying: *mine*
as we rode toward flame with the sky in our mouths—
the trees turning gold, then crimson, white

and the heart saying: *mine*
of the wild, bright world;
the trees turning gold, then crimson, white
as they burned in the darkness, and we were girls

of the wild, bright world
of the woods near our house—we could turn, see the lights
as they burned in the darkness, and we were girls
so we rode just to ride

through the woods near our house—we could turn, see the lights—
and the horses would carry us, carry us home
so we rode just to ride,
my sister and I, just to be close to the danger of love

and the horses would carry us, carry us home
—two borrowed horses, two local boys,
my sister and I—just to be close to that danger, desire—
one night, bareback and young, we rode through the woods.

(2003)

CATHERINE BOWMAN (BORN 1957)

∾

Demographics

They don't want to stop. They can't stop.
　　They've been going at it for days now,
for hours, for months, for years. He's on top
　　of her. She's on top of him. He's licking
her between the legs. Her fingers
　　are in his mouth. It's November.
It's March. It's July and there are palms.
　　Palms and humidity. It's the same man.
It's a different man. It's August and slabs
　　of heat waves wallow on tarred lots.
Tornadoes sprawl across open plains.
　　Temperatures rise. Rains accumulate.
Somewhere a thunderstorm dies. Somewhere
　　a snow falls, colored by the red dust
of a desert. She spreads her legs. His lips
　　suck her nipples. She smells his neck.
It's morning. It's night. It's noon.
　　It's this year. It's last year. It's 4 a.m.
It started when the city shifted growth
　　to the north, over the underground
water supply. Now the back roads are gone
　　where they would drive, the deer glaring into
the headlights, Wetmore and Thousand Oaks,
　　and the ranch roads that led to the hill country
and to a trio of deep-moving rivers.
　　There were low-water crossings. Flood gauges.
Signs for falling rock. There were deer blinds
　　for sale. There was cedar in the air.
Her hands are on his hips. He's pushing
　　her up and down. There are so many things
she's forgotten. The names of trees. Wars.
　　Recipes. The trench graves filled with hundreds.

Was it Bolivia? Argentina? Chile?
    Was it white gladioli that decorated the altar
where wedding vows were said? There was
    a dance floor. Tejano classics.
A motel. A shattered mirror. Flies.
    A Sunbelt sixteen-wheeler. Dairy Queens.
Gas stations. The smells of piss and cement.
    There was a field of corn, or was it cotton?
There were yellow trains and silver silos.
    They can't stop. They don't want to stop.
It's spring, and five billion inhale
    and exhale across two hemispheres. Oceans
form currents and countercurrents.
    There was grassland. There was sugar cane.
There were oxen. Metallic ores.
    There was Timber. Fur-bearing animals.
Rice lands. Industry. Tundra. Winds
    cool the earth's surface. Thighs press
against thighs. Levels of water fluctuate.
    And yesterday a lightning bolt reached
a temperature hotter than the sun.

(1993)

ED SMITH (1957–2005)

Poem

I reached into his pajamas and put my hand on his little
cock—only it wasn't so little! As a matter of fact it was
over eight feet long! "How can your dick be so big and still fit
in your pj's?" I asked suggestively. "Well, you know, it's all
magic," he replied quizzically.

The head of his penis parted my pussy lips irrationally.
Since his dick is eight feet long and I'm only five-two it had to
go somewhere. I felt his rock-hard boyhood filling up my
insides, then I felt his force parting my tonsils then
pressing the back of my teeth.

Like a tulip in the spring, or maybe a marigold—nay—a
sunflower! his head emerged from my head. It was so long
it was sticking a foot and a half out of my mouth yet he
was sitting across the room in the rocking chair.

I reached up and started stroking his shaft with my hands
wet with my saliva and pussy juices gentle at first then
with increasing vigor. Finally he came like an epileptic
firehose pulsating up through my entire being. His cum
literally soaked the floor but every drop missed me. It was
the best safe sex I ever had.

(c. 1986–1987)

༚

How to Have an Orgasm: Examples

In ancient Greece, it was the object of a young woman to seduce a god. Warm summer days, nubile maidens lay nude in the meadows or on the beaches, legs parted as they waited for clouds, birds or bulls to descend upon them. To capture a god in orgasm could cause immortality or earthquakes.

In Barbados, orgasms are known to take on the dimensions of houses. Some are claustrophobic cottages inhabited by insomniacs, some are castles ruled by the strict orders of bitchy queens, while others are multi-storied hotels with visitors from all over the world. In the lobby of the hotels women discuss the theater and model the latest styles in fur coats and lingerie while in the background an orchestra plays the *1812 Overture.*

After death, a monogamous man is forced to sit with his late, beloved wife and watch reruns of the movies his mind played in their most intimate moments.

All orgasms are actors and actresses. While some orgasms deliver soliloquies, others glide noiselessly across the blond carpet of your skin.

On cool autumn evenings, on the highways of Virginia, a woman races her black Corvette. Close behind her a police car whines, red lights flashing. Before the night is over, the woman with jet-black hair will be held in the arms of a moaning sheriff, tire tracks and skid marks embedded in one another's flesh and dreams.

At Himalayan altitudes, orgasms are rare, occur in different colors and float off without us as puffy clouds. Sometimes couples sigh and admire a luminescent pink orgasm as it vanishes into the horizon. Other times a woman stares accusingly at her lover while pointing to a vile, gray plume, *Is that the best you can do?*

Some orgasms can devour you. They are wild animals that need to be civilized. After a minute with such an orgasm, your insides are gnawed by tiny teeth.

In a tearoom in Manhattan, a fortune-teller was reading the lines of a young man's hand when she saw he would be besieged by admiring women. Each woman would be a musician and would play his body as her preferred instrument. For some he would be a drum. For others, a mandolin. Alas, he had always wanted to be a violin, but fate would have it that he wouldn't meet the woman who would see him as a violin until he was an old man and had given up on women.

Maybe you are a stranger in your own orgasm. You wander through it, cool and unmoved, feeling like a burglar or a Peeping Tom. You watch yourself, feeling more and more anxious, sweating profusely, fearing you will be caught, someone will know the truth. You are but a voyeur of orgasms.

(1993)

I See a Man

He has just had sex. I can tell by the way, when he
notices his shadow ahead of him, broad, spilling over both
curbs to the road he is walking down slowly, most of him
wants to stop and, as if remembering, stand briefly at a
kind of attention. He has just had sex, it's unclear with
whom. It was a man, it was a woman . . . it was the air, whose
inconveniently wide-apart edges can be all day coming together.
There's this sense in which it can't matter—sex being,
for him, any attempt to fill a space in so there's no room
left, for a while, for what he surely calls a suffering inside
him—that much his brow gives away, his mouth too, designed,
it seems, for delivering lines like *Already, as far into
the world as I've wanted, I've come.* He's thirty, thirty-two—
it's easy, still, to say a thing like that. Write it down,
even. Call it a poem.

(1995)

༜

House-Sitting

She lies on her girlfriend's bed looking at the pictures in her girl-friend's husband's *Playboy*. The big artificial breasts like glazed holiday breads on the cover of *Family Circle*. It's all the same: the body varnish that glistens women and turkeys, that sells them. This is how she feels about it politically anyway—angry, threatened, misrepresented. But her clit begins rising against her will, like a new tooth through resistant gum, and she hates her body for being aroused, her own skin soft and spread, a dull white finish, poultry before it's cooked, something no one would want to buy or eat.

She looks at these airbrushed computerized pinups, fleshy robots, pouting like she never sees anyone pout on the street. Even though they are all the same, she likes some of them more than others, their ass cheeks smooth as marbles, forgiving her for her own, lumpy as golf balls. She tries to imagine their personalities, maybe some are smart or funny or clumsy.

She cannot quite dream she is one of them as she lies on those thick quilts, with her girlfriend's red high heels and her girlfriend's husband's denim work shirt. She cannot quite dream that she's lying above a caption for phone sex: *I'm wet, I'm horny, give me a call.* And she knows she couldn't enjoy touching such rubbery slick skin, which looks as though it would be cold and indifferent, like the pages of the magazine itself. What is the proper response of a woman looking at *Playboy*? Why did she bring it with her to lie on the bed? Is her friend upset with her husband when he does? Why does her whole body blush, her stomach warm—one mouth a little wet, the other a little dry.

She hadn't looked at a magazine like this since sixth grade, for which anyone would have forgiven her. But now, as a grown woman, why does she touch one of her own breasts, losing, for just a second, her disappointment in its lack of firmness, still looking at the Bunnies—

all cupcakes and maraschino cherries — stomachs as flat as Pop-Tarts, their fingernails, little pink wings. She parts the hair that tangles over her vulva. Her orgasm is quick and salty, forgettable as fast food. What she does with the magazine is what she guesses any man does — put it back exactly where it was hidden, then sleep away the guilt, the shame.

(1994)

At Seventeen

I want to do it, want to snort and root
and forage in your skin and apertures.
It happens fast. It hits a frantic pitch.

I want to touch touch, suck suck, lick lick
like my kin in the animal kingdom.
Suction noises horrify and thrill me,

forensic evidence of what I'm doing
and doing and doing, pants around
my ankles, wigs in my hair. I am

sweaty and dirty, a little bit bloody,
smell of exactly what I have been
up to, sneak home like the criminal I am,

new memory like a seltzer in my crotch.

(1991)

Francesca Says More

that maiden thump *was* book on floor, but
does it really matter who kissed who
first or then who decided to go further?
lower? faster? naturally, we took
turns on top. *now here, now there, and up*
and down . . . once it started no one even thought to think to stop.
so, we have holes inside our souls,
but mustn't we begin by filling others'?
god gave us lips and hands and parts
that cannot possibly be saved for prayer. nor by.
i will not name name, claim fame by how well
or who i fucked or why, it happens all the time.
and it's you, white pilgrim, whom next galehot seeks.

fuck. we didn't read again for weeks.

(And More)

(o (l)uxu/orious (p)/(l)ussuria) one can rule
rimini and still not rule (or rim) me. doric, ionic,
phallic: i liked it all. i moaned and wept as i do now,
but it was a joy and a different kind of sorrow:
to see your lover's eyes when he's down there. down there
the very root *was* the very root, and fig was fruit and nut
gelato. down here how it happened can still make me shudder.
sigh.
just how far down, sinner, must you go? whatever pleases you:
follow my tail, my thigh. and: VIDE FICA MIA. eat my furbellowed
heart, tremble at my furbo and my body gone but still beautiful
heart, this life that's for the birds is saved by rhyming such as our
heart, if you twist my arm just right i'll lose my mind.

the new style is the old style: from behind.

Francesca Says Too Much

each day i came an infinity of times; it rained and reign
was so complete with every pleasure as if in love i sang.
pity you're confused: 'twasn't love, it was sex that dissolved me:
limo was body and mud. and long and shiny
and briny what i polished with my tongue marmo hard and pallina
smooth once whetted i never stopped saying sipa, was always in
position, in the mood, too much was never enough. i kept open
my arms my legs my eyes my lips moving lifted to heaven
my ass my hips. pilgrim, can you picture it? my tits. and it was
all wet. don't cry. dry your ablutionary tears. no thing now can absolve me
but i regret it not: i was so alive! o, to again have
someone's occhi and fingers and penes on in me, to be
licked and sucked and eaten and fucked and debauched.

sigh and sign and eye hungry pilgrim, if only you could have watched.

Francesca Can Too Stop Thinking About Sex, Reflect upon Her Position in Poetry, Write a Real Sonnet.

pilgrim, i did not mean to be so loose
of tongue, so bold in all i loosely told
in my smut so smug, so overly sold.
i did not mean, pilgrim, to traduce.

i apologize, i offer no excuse:
but, poet, though you have right to scold
it was highsouled you who made my mouth hold
what it held and tell what it told. a truce,

no, let's call it an honor. mine is apt,
as far as long sentences go: my vice
in your verse will tempt others to try

and sing: readers, lovers forever rapt
and about to sweetly sigh: paradise!
thank you, poet, for keeping me alive.

(2006)

Preference

Some people need a harsher kind of love.
I like the smooth soft wetness of our sex.
I like the gentle easy way we move,

our bodies blending in a fleshy weave,
our lips, torsos, tongues a sensuous mix.
Some people need a harsher kind of love.

One plays the master, the other plays the slave.
They plunge each other's depths with plastic dicks.
I like him gentle. I like his easy move

against me, desire rising like a wave
that draws us slowly to its crest then breaks.
Some women need a harsher kind of love.

A brutish forceful man is what they crave.
They scream and bite; they claw their lovers' backs.
I like the gentle, easy way you move,

and taste and touch my skin, without a glove,
or ropes to bind me. How could I relax,
confronted with a harsher kind of love?
I'll take the gentle, easy way we move.

(1996)

On Not Using the Word "Cunt" in a Poem

Certainly there's pressure to perform
in such a way what doesn't sound so stately
and isn't safe: *Let it be shorn,*

the poem's lush holiness. Let locks be trimmed.
Cut to the chase. How unchaste can you be?
Can I proffer a different kind of tongue,

one that licks nether regions? Can I start
offering words that aren't courtly or cute
and don't contain such blanket recanting

of words I use when I am in a wreck
or mad at somebody or being fucked
—those anti-canticles I chant when hurt,

the kind of words I punt when breaking glass
or bumping ceilings? Can I be curt,
not hunt for language so gosh-darned appealing

but pick what's more intransigent
and less ornate? Or is that just a judgment
ignorance can make—that stealing

the spotlight, showing one can "rough it up"
is really more mere decorativeness,
like the performance of a burlesque romp

by someone who would rather keep her dress?
Is that all poems can do to snatch attention,
use such dim tents of tricks? Let's nick

this baby in the bud: am I too mendicant
to fluid cadence? Do I serve lip
by thinking a poem is holy, not a hole

to thrust things in, for the very sake of thrusting?
Or do I suit myself for an audience
by shirking my naked voice, or the cliché

of what a woman's naked utterance
would be, as if just honest women cussed?
Should I be someone who docks elegance

because it's penal territory,
someone who takes the name of poetry
in vain—who kicks the ass of beauty?

I know we're all voyeurs, but can't
you come for me a different way this time
and listen, for one minute, to a poem

that's not revealing crotch and pay attention?
Is it impossible for me to strut
my stuff without the madonna/whore

dichotomy? Without the flash of tit
-illation, would you give my poem a date?
Or must I count my kind of cunning out?

(2005)

August in West Hollywood

All day I watch the neighbor's boy
paint the side of his house.

He seems to rest so easily on the ladder rungs,
shirtless, lanky-limbed, hips tilting in the sun.

In the morning, I am the house, blueing beneath his brushstrokes,
each rib a shingle, my breasts, windowpanes, my waist,

the broad wood planks flattening beneath his brushstrokes,
my shoulders, shutters, lips and eyelashes fluttering eaves.

By four, I'm the roller brush,
turned and turning in his working hands.

Come dusk, I'm the open pail of paint
beside him on the grass—wide-mouthed, emptied.

The neighbor's house breathes in its new skin beneath the streetlamp.
It puts its face to the darkness and does not recognize itself.

(2004)

❧

When a man hasn't been kissed

When I haven't been kissed in a long time,
I walk behind well-dressed women
on cold December mornings and shovel
the steamy exhalations pluming from their lips
down my throat with both hands, hoping
a single molecule will cling to my lungs.

I sneak into the ladies' room of a fancy
restaurant, dig in the trashcan for a napkin
where a woman checked her lipstick,
then go home, light candles, put on Barry White,
and gently press the napkin all over my body.

I think leeches are the most romantic creatures
because all they want to do is kiss. If only
someone invented a kinder, gentler leech,
I'd paint it bright pink and pretend
Winona Ryder's lips crawled off her face,
up my thigh, and were sucking on my swollen

bicep. When I haven't been kissed,
I create civil disturbances, then insult
the cops who show up, till one grabs me
by the collar and hurls me against the squad car,
so I can remember, at least for a moment,
what it's like to be touched.

(2002)

RICHARD SIKEN (BORN 1967)

∾

Little Beast

1

all-night barbeque. A dance on the courthouse lawn.
    The radio aches a little tune that tells the story of what the night
hinking. It's thinking of love.
                    It's thinking of stabbing us to death
I leaving our bodies in a dumpster.
    That's a nice touch, stains in the night, whiskey and kisses for everyone.

night, by the freeway, a man eating fruit pie with a buckknife
    carves the likeness of his lover's face into the motel wall. I like him
I I want to be like him, my hands no longer an afterthought.

2

neone once told me that explaining is an admission of failure.
    I'm sure you remember, I was on the phone with you, sweetheart.

3

story repeats itself. Somebody says this.
    History throws its shadow over the beginning, over the desktop,
r the sock drawer with its socks, its hidden letters.
              History is a little man in a brown suit
    trying to define a room he is outside of.
now history. There are many names in history
                    but none of them are ours.

4

had green eyes,
        so I wanted to sleep with him—
green eyes flecked with yellow, dried leaves on the surface of a pool—

You could drown in those eyes, I said.
                                    The fact of his pulse,
the way he pulled his body in, out of shyness or shame or a desire
        not to disturb the air around him.
Everyone could see the way his muscles worked,
                        the way we look like animals,
                                    his skin barely keeping him inside
            I wanted to take him home
and rough him up and get my hands inside him, drive my body into his
        like a crash test car.
                        I wanted to be wanted and he was
very beautiful, kissed with his eyes closed, and only felt good while moving.
        You could drown in those eyes, I said,
                                    so it's summer, so it's suicide,
so we're helpless in sleep and struggling at the bottom of the pool.

                                5

It wasn't until we were well past the middle of it
        that we realized
the old dull pain, whose stitched wrists and clammy fingers,
                                    far from being subverted,
had only slipped underneath us, freshly scrubbed.
                    Mirrors and shopwindows returned our faces to us,
            replete with the tight lips and the eyes that remained eyes
                        and not the doorways we had hoped fo
His wounds healed, the skin a bit thicker than before,
        scars like train tracks on his arms and on his body underneath his shirt.

                                6

We still groped for each other on the back stairs or in parked cars
                                    as the roads around
grew glossy with ice and our breath softened the view through a glass
            already laced with frost,
but more frequently I was finding myself sleepless, and he was running out c
                                    lullabies.
But damn if there isn't anything sexier
                    than a slender boy with a handgun,
                            a fast car, a bottle of pill

hat would you like? I'd like my money's worth.

　　　　　　　　Try explaining a life bundled with episodes of this—
　swallowing mud, swallowing glass, the smell of blood
the first four knuckles.

　　　　　　　　　　We pull our boots on with both hands
t we can't punch ourselves awake and all I can do
　　　is stand on the curb and say *Sorry*
　　　　　　　about the blood in your mouth. I wish it was mine.

ouldn't get the boy to kill me, but I wore his jacket for the longest time.

(2000)

JENNIFER L. KNOX (BORN 1968)

Another Motive for Metaphor

I love to masturbate, especially
After a poem of mine's accepted in
A literary magazine. Shit—
I open up that letter, smile awhile
And think, "This one goes out to Don, a total
Tool who I temped for in '89:
Data-mother-fucking-entry *this.*"
Who's got "inappropriate footwear" now?
"The inappropriate footwear's on the other
Foot today, you hick," I tell him, tell
Them all, as, lifting up my shirt, I notice
Nipples! Mine (O, gorgeous areolas!—
Pink as peonies)! And ass (my bouncy
Pony, prance in skintight smarty-pants!)!

(2005)

JANICE ERLBAUM (BORN 1969)

∾

The Temp

He's in love with you. But you're only his
For the workweek. At night, you're married.
On weekends, you lie with your husband
And tell him you're thinking about work.
How his hands make things move across his desk.
How he signs his e-mails. He adores you.

Everyone knows about the two of you,
Though nothing's happened, of course, you're his
Colleague. So what if you stop by his desk
To say, I'm hungry. Are you absolutely married
To the idea of pizza? I propose let's work
On it later. The phone rings. It's your husband.

Like a man from TV, your husband
Doesn't exist in your real life, you
Can't seem to place him when you're at work.
A staticky shape in the mist; his
Sheepish face, the reason you married
Him, a bent paper clip in your desk.

Chastely, your lover stops by your desk.
Stop calling him that. You have a husband.
And everyone knows you're married
To the job. So concentrate. He tells you
He's written the perfect agenda; this, his
Persistent attempt to woo you through work.

He has become your husband at work.
The dry marital bed of his desk
Where you reach for the comfort of his
Desire. You need another husband,

A partner, someone to bear fruit with you.
He pines for you. You crave it. Thus, you're married.

You'll never leave the man you married
For the man that you married at work.
You don't have to. He belongs to you,
Like the menu you stow in your desk.
Like dessert. You don't tell your husband.
It's not cheating. Just, this business isn't his.

His hand touches yours. Whose? Their faces, married
Into one face, one husband, one unending job to work.
The desk is your bed, the bed your desk. And the dutiful bride—that's you.

(2004)

Misapprehension

I don't want you always to act your age:
Fall apart a little for me, please,
so when I kiss your mouth, your brow, your creamy
arms, your downy neck, eyelids, your strange
intense dark copper-lidded eyes that close
against me, when I hold you till your whole
strut-length of spine releases to my holding,
when I lay you, stroke your guiltless rose
open toward me, ages overturned . . .
I don't want you to act your age, just yearn
toward what I offer; soften to my touch,
let me reach the place where you give milk,
suck and tongue you till my touch is much,
much more than youth or age or silk on silk.

(2000)

CATE MARVIN (BORN 1969)

Me and Men

The soiled fists of socks shucked before
     they fell lumbersome to bed, the dirty pans,
        the glasses their lips kissed fisted soapy
   in my sink-worn hands. The flea-seeded sink,
      basin of stubble shorn, their low snores
        rumbling nights long as freight trains.

True, some nights their eyes pooled with light,
     cleared to brown, unmuddied their river bottoms.
        But more often, I liked best not being with them,
     driving alone and thinking only of the fact of them.
       Their flat bodies I held with grave disrespect;
          perhaps this is why I sought them.

There were shadows beneath their eyes, and sweet
     and slow moments unzipping their flies. I may
        have gasped from time to time. But it is unfortunate,
   for my men, that they knew me, and I knew them
      as men. My blankness should have never
        had anything to do with them. I tried

to forgive them for dropping their dirty clothes
     by the bed, for playing deaf to my questions,
        for ashing on my favorite rug, for slamming doors
   on my hands, for being them. I can't blame them
      for owning what I wanted, back when
        what I wanted was had only by men.

If I can't wish a scar away, how can I wish them
     obliviated from my touching? The fact is,
        I am unable to remember their faces, any
   of them, the smell of their collars, the fury I felt,

208

why I broke and broke things. It all seems quite bland,
and I would rather think of animals I have had.

(2001)

CATHERINE WAGNER (BORN 1969)

❧

Lover

Prince Genji was in love with me in the eleventh century. Put his hand through my screens. Why Lady Murasaki you may go.

Sir Walter Scott courted me wi' glove and ring, wi' brotch and knife. I said you faker.

Sartre I fucked, it was bad.

Djuna Barnes was in love with me I told her I was scared she said Lie down!

Byron said he was we only flirted.

Will you said Lady Mary Wortley Montague stay after tea. Your ankle my dear as you rose from the clavichord.

Your hair being of the softest brightness and your bosom of the brightest softness I am loath to choose between and must address myself to both—so Philip Sidney

Once sat on Wystan Auden's lap—kissed his jaw and rubbed his belly. I stuck my hand in his pants and found his old thing. We were both delighted. "Hag," he said.

Job I said God punish you for a righteous man I am raw.

Come in while I dress. I will not, said Charlotte Brontë and waited in the snow.

Virginia W and I bathing—neglected pond. A honeybee pricked my lower thigh. Quoth she, where the bee suck—

(1997)

C. DALE YOUNG (BORN 1969)

∾

Maelstrom

Wind shook the trees and rain crackled
at the windows. Could it have been
any other way? Rain coming down,
clothes wet, water dripping from our hair?

At the window, could it have been
a ghost singing its final warning?
Clothes wet, water dripping from our hair,
he fell on me like rain. I could not speak.

A ghost sang its final warning
like a storm. He tore my shirt open
and fell on me like rain. I could not speak,
and I closed my eyes. It started like this.

Like a storm, he tore my shirt open,
the light in the stairwell flickering
as I closed my eyes. It started like this:
the steps pressing into my back,

the light in the stairwell flickering
sensing storm, our hands trembling.
The steps pressed into my back
under the sound of belts unbuckling.

Sensing storm, our hands trembled.
I could not watch, could not speak.
Under the sound of belts unbuckling,
a future unraveled like spun gold.

I could not watch, could not speak
then. And now, years later, the same

future unravels like spun gold:
the arguments, the body's betrayals.

Then and now, years later, the same
quiet lying about the house.
The arguments, the body's betrayals
resist closure or the quick dismissal.

This quiet lies about my house.
Again wind shakes the trees and rain crackles.
You resist closure or the quick dismissal.
Rain coming down. It started like this.

(2002)

∾

Voluptuary

Normal love begs for kink. Loving wrong
is twisted and hair, the hair of blood-timed
mammals and damsels in paintings curls
subversively without effort.

And espionage of flesh roots in the dirt
of the heart. Vinegar love floods the tongue
with a uriny fire and who argues? Sour aunts.
In lovers' mouths, only saccharine is unholy.

And if my sister married now then I will
wed wonder, I will seek blunder,
and wifely be naked for a throttled,
verging slumber slit with: love is losing.

If you haven't known the true faulty
pleasure of half-beauty, the sublime uncomely,
dreamt without vision two hot marble arches
round your vague orca trumpet of a thigh,

then why would you love me? And how does
fever break without liquid, without spilling?
What woman cannot speak of strumpets? Who
has struck the head of lust without a strain?

Where is the mark, the dark, the brain?
I want terror only listening for the shallows
in the shame. Like dancers, elasticized time
for the sake of the body. And what body?

Blister, wizen. It's worth it and it's night.
Who wants pretty, when pretty is plain

and the heart is gnarled and the fullsaked
forest of being lost is home?

Forest where we love the beast surprising.
Anticipated fetish like missing toes. Or a thick,
dark, hairy heart, full to pluck or comb.
Or old. Where is the old, old lover;

finally ripe enough to fall without falling?
What is blossoming
when the darker sun inside feeds
the silence of starker stars?

(1999)

Étude

I love making
love most just

after—adrift—
the cries & sometime

tears over, our strong
swimming done—

sheet wreck—
mattress a life-

boat, listing—

(2003)

JILL ALEXANDER ESSBAUM (BORN 1971)

On Reading Poorly Transcribed Erotica

She stood before him wearing only pantries
and he groped for her Volvo under the gauze.
She had saved her public hair, and his cook
went hard as a fist. They fell to the bad.
He shoveled his duck into her posse
and all her worm juices spilled out.
Still, his enormous election raged on.
Her beasts heaved as he sacked them,
and his own nibbles went stuff as well.
She put her tong in his rear and talked ditty.
Oh, it was all that he could do not to comb.

(2004)

BETH ANN FENNELLY (BORN 1971)

Why We Shouldn't Write Love Poems, or If
We Must, Why We Shouldn't Publish Them

How silly Robert Lowell seems in *Norton's*,
all his love vows on facing pages: his second wife,
who simmered like a wasp, his third,
the dolphin who saved him, even "Skunk Hour"
for Miss Bishop (he proposed though she was gay),
and so on, a ten-page manic zoo of love,
he should have praised less and bought a dog.

We fall in love, we fumble for a pen,
we send our poems out like Jehovah's Witnesses—
in time they return home, and when they do
they find the locks changed, FOR SALE stabbed in the yard.
Oh, aren't the poems stupid and devout,
trying each key in their pockets in plain view
of the neighbors, some of whom openly gloat.

We should write about what we know
won't change, volleyball, Styrofoam, or mildew.
If I want to write about our picnic in Alabama,
I should discuss the red-clay earth or fire ants,
not what happened while we sat cross-legged there
leaning over your surprise for me, crawfish you'd boiled with—
surprise again—three times too much crab boil—

Oh, how we thumbed apart the perforated joints
and scooped the white flesh from the red parings,
blowing on our wet hands between bites
because they burned like stars. Afterward,
in the public park, in hot sun, on red clay, inside my funnel
of thighs and skirt, your spicy, burning fingers shucked

the shell of my panties, then found my sweet meat
and strummed it, until it too was burning, burning, burning—

Ah, poem, I am weak from love, and you,
you are sneaky. Do not return home to shame me.

(2004)

Preface

Well, ain't your mouth a pretty little pace-
maker. And *mmmm* that tongue is a carp
I'd sure like to harpoon! We could eat crêpe-
suzettes in the dim café
below your hypothalamus. I'd pull the last pear
from the pear tree. We could peer
over the ridge of your throat or creep
down the ladder until we reached the reef.
But before setting forth, you should accept whatever's free
because, Baby, I've got at least an acre
of desires you can reap.

(2001)

Eye-Fucked

for CW, the younger

You were just my candy, sweet-tart,
a skittle in the corner of the bar.
I caught you with a dance
and swung you on a star.
You were Mr. Good,
a hardheaded-honey that I bit
while on the beach under a wink
of moon. Soon even the waves
exchanged their tune—a snicker
for a swoon. Is the question:
did we swim or did we sink?
Were we suckerfish who struck out
on the sand? (Did we let things
get in and out of hand?)
Or was it just the glint of a passing
disco-eye-ball that cast its spark
and shadow before leading me
down your hall? Help me dove,
my dog-and-pony show's
all laced up in a licorice whip.
Is the flicker of an eye all that love
is made of? A tickle blink of
sweet and spice, just a hint
of lark? Love, I made my eyes for you,
and you, love, you keep
this retina in the dark.

(2006)

❧

Body Cavity

You have the right to remain silent.

A videotape recording of this procedure shall be made.

Videotaping shall begin as soon as my search begins. I shall first state the date and time, clearly, and the camera operator shall then enter this information electronically onto the videotape.

The camera operator during your strip search shall be of the same sex you are, unless you request otherwise. This option may not be possible in some areas.

During this search, assuming compliancy, a privacy barrier (e.g., curtain, wall, sheet, screen, door, cardboard, beach towel, piece of wood, office cubicle divider or any other similar barrier preventing visual inspection of the private parts) shall be placed between you and the camera operator. If compliancy is not assured and/or there is the threat of your physical resistance, camera operators are instructed to videotape both you and the officer conducting the search simultaneously to protect against allegations of improper physical interactions, in which case all or partial nudity may be captured on videotape.

The purpose of this search will be stated just before it is to begin. There is some evidence that needs to be obtained. While conducting the search of your body, I shall, when possible, wear gloves. If it is not possible to wear gloves, I shall wash my hands thoroughly before returning to work. Then I shall wash them again.

You will be asked to hand over any hazardous materials before the search begins. Failure to do so could result in hazardous conditions for you and for me.

You will shake your hair vigorously. You will lean forward slightly against a stable countertop or the hood of an official vehicle. I will stand slightly to one side of your body. I will begin to search your hair and your head. I will run my fingers through your hair. If you prefer to run your own fingers through your hair, that's okay too, and I will watch this.

Next, I will inspect your nasal, ear and mouth cavities, including the crevice behind your ear. You will lift your hair up off your neck. If you have any false teeth, you will need to remove them now.

You will stand with your arms extended, fingers spread. I will unfold your collar, cuffs, sleeves and any other creases found in your clothing. I will squeeze your collar. I will run my hands over your shoulder and down the length of your arms, down to your hands, then back up and into your armpits. I will unbutton your shirt and pay special attention to your armpits, the small of your back, your chest.

You will be taken to a more private area, where you will be asked to remove your bra and lean forward. I will take hold of the center of your bra and shake it. I will instruct you to lift your breasts so that I may inspect under them.

I will descend to your waistband. I will run my hands over it and squeeze it. I will unbuckle you, unbutton you. I will run my hands along your waist and proceed then to the buttocks and legs. Your legs will be slightly apart. I will unzip your pants or skirt. I will be using both hands at this juncture. I will be paying special attention to the seams. As I check each leg, I will check the crotch area. I will run my hand well up into the groin.

I will instruct you to squat down and cough. This will permit me a visual check of your darker areas.

Where possible, I will use tongs or forceps to assist me in difficult-to-reach areas.

Then I will switch to the other side of your body, conditions permitting, and repeat the procedure from step one, methodically and with great care, this time more familiar with the curvature of your body, the nature of its hiding places.

I will proceed as quickly as I'm comfortable, and with sensitivity to the subtle responses I provoke in you. What items I find during the search will be placed in my plastic evidence bag.

We shall begin the search now. The time is midnight.

(2003)

Reverence

Love not the rider but the old rider,
The ghost in the saddle: Obey that ghost.
A good horse runs even at the shadow of the whip.
But we are not good horses.
We bolt. We stand still in bad weather.
We rely on things we know are unreliable,
It feels so good just to *rely*.
We are relied on.
But I don't know who knows that bad secret.
I don't see who sits astride my back,
Who cuts my flank so lovingly on our way to the dark mountain.

(2006)

RAVI SHANKAR (BORN 1975)

Lucia

My hair, voluminous from sleeping in
six different positions, redolent with your scent,
helps me recall that last night was indeed real,

that it's possible for a bedspread to spawn
a watershed in the membrane that keeps us
shut in our own skins, mute without pleasure,

that I didn't just dream you into being.
You fit like a fig in the thick of my tongue,
give my hands their one true purpose,

find in my shoulder a groove for your head.
In a clinch, you're clenched and I'm pinched,
we're spooned, forked, wrenched, lynched

in a chestnut by a mob of our own making,
only to be resurrected to stage several revivals
that arise from slightest touch to thwart

deep sleep with necessities I never knew
I knew until meeting you a few days
or many distant, voluptuous lifetimes ago.

(2005)

From the Other

What is small is smaller, suddenly.
Her shoulder, small, with my hand on it,
her ferociousness is something I can grip.
I am so hungry for anything. Blind.

With her breast on my chest, my blindness
finds its course, surging. She is what I am surging
towards, through, pushing in makes her beauty
fragment, disperse, hover.

Pushing freely now. The resistance
her body makes, it is the resistance
air makes for a wounded flyer.
Won't she take me in farther?

(2005)

DANIELLE PAFUNDA (BORN 1977)

∽

Courtesy

I took a bite from the wormy part for the cur in my stomach.
My plastic, my porcelain stomach. My lover, he wore a buzzer
in the palm of his heart. A hot rod. My lover was a dry heave.
I pinned my hair for him, with a bat bone. I pinned the page
to the wall of the discount drugstore. An advertisement for tricks.

They put the broads on a broad street and the clinicians above
the drugstore. The deference to the white coat and round eye
of the stethoscope. The chill in my lover's fingers was a false
negative. A falsie. I took a pint for the first five days and
a pint-point-five for the rest.

I slit my skirt. I slit the turf around my garden bed. I lay it
with torn news and vegetable scraps. I lit my tongue in the slit
of an envelope. A reverse. A recipe inside. My lover wore
chef's gloves, for fighting the eager meat. For the quick
he cut me.

(2004)

❧

February

Imagine, if you must, another man;
he'll imagine me. I'll touch you
with his foreign hands; you'll feel he
is sweeter, softer. I'll feel strange
inside you as a stranger; you will feel
better with another for your lover.
I'll imagine you, your usual mouth;
your tongue will be unusual between
his different lips. I'll feel your kiss
as an offense; he'll punish your
perversity, but I will come
to your defense. Then you will come
to his: that criminal whose fingerprints,
blushing on your breast, resemble mine.

(2006)

Sonnet from the Groin

Crazed with spring all I want to do is fuck, free
these thighs their denim prison, let the rich
scent floating around my neck take a look see
into the under things of a man. (Which
man is a trivial spec.) Oh! To be flying
above a mattress, screaming not with hate
but with throaty mating only trying
for the peak and pinnacle of frolic. Fate
and I have made a bargain: to compel
the most virile to lay me down, discipline
the demon out of my body. Possible
friction, find me I'm not hiding, will become
an electric pink rubber band on command. Womb
you have nothing to do with this! Time to bloom.

(2007)

∾

Valentine

I love the word *fuck*, how he grazes
my teeth, scrapes, stabs at my tongue
like a fork, first kiss, valentine red
hatchet, how desperately he wants
out, wishbone lodged in my throat,
werewolf loose in the suburbs, goes
wherever, cold gallon of milk glugging
across the Formica countertop, warm
scissors wandering through sheet metal
or sequined curtains of striated muscle,
is easy to use, aim and fire, operates
without AA batteries or ever suddenly
going soft, how the other words
in the locker room hate him, lone
paddleboat gliding amongst a pack
of unforgivably smug canoes,
icicle pitted against a tray of ice cubes,
cheerfully recruited, frogman overboard
out of my mouth into its next mission,
surefire blades of a ceiling fan spinning
in your swaggering den of blue-sleeved
parakeets.

(2007)

∽

Letter to My Love

Dear lord, you are no backbreaking orchid.
You will give that man your last dollar.
When I meet you, lord, I curtsy, chop and mitigate
the customs, and you, my muff-diving butternut
go whooping through the corridor like it's the last
day of summer and you're Mr. Moneybags
reminding us all to tread sloppy water.
Lord, I saw the kettles gather in the stonefields.
I saw the meniscus fall asleep.
When the masons shook their glory
from their bright and feathered hairdos
I turned away, lord, turned to see you
gallop down the highway. Where were you
headed? Even now, a light-year
from that beating, I want to know.

(2005)

Subterranean Gnomesick Blues; or,
the Gnome Who Whet My Fleshy Tent.

In lands where the waters are clear
And the forests virginal, where the heavens
Are full only of birds and stars—
Before writing a poem about it, I find it helpful to masturbate.
I believe this is also true of camping,
For there is no privacy once you pitch the tent.

Indeed, I had pitched a bonny tent
And my next task soon was clear;
Hastily I had gone off camping
And beard of Zeus! My sainted heavens!
I had completely forgotten to masturbate!
So thus I lay, and, twitching 'neath the stars,

I saw, beneath my eyelids, a host of stars
Of pornographic nature— But ho! A rustling in my tent!
Oh go away! Can't you see I'm trying to masturbate!
And in the corner, 'twas all too clear
As I raised my fist to curse the heavens—
A gnome stood setting up his gear for camping.

"Sorry to disturb you while you're . . . *camping*,"
Said he dryly, his gray eyes twinkling stars.
"It seems I am drawn here by the heavens
Here to make my home inside this tent,
For to the nose of a gnome there is nothing more clear
Than the scent of a woman as she masturbates."

He dropped his tiny drawers to masturbate
And, as he did, I forgot all about camping.
Confused I was, but in sooth, one thing was clear—

This gnome's cock could threaten all the stars
Of my earlier fantasy; and what good's a tent
If not to screw a gnome preordained by the heavens?

And so smiled the heavens!
And no longer had I need to masturbate!
And so his red-coned hat tore through my tent!
And so blew up his pouch of things for camping!
For small Gnostic/Gnomic/Paracelsian lovers come to us like stars
And we must take away our fingers to make their entry clear.

No longer can I masturbate unless I think of camping—
What cursed stars, what blasphemous heavens
On a clear night sent a priapic gnome into my tent.

(2004)

Contributors were asked to name their favorite work of erotic writing—any genre, any language—and to comment briefly on the choice. Assisted by Jill Baron, David Lehman wrote the notes for the deceased contributors.

Kim Addonizio was born in Washington, D.C., in 1954. Her most recent book of poems is *What Is This Thing Called Love* (W. W. Norton, 2004).

"I haven't read much erotica, but I'd have to say that *The Story of O* made quite an impression. I think the reasons I like it had best remain private. Also, the writing is very vivid."

Ai was born in Albany, Texas, in 1947. Her most recent book is *Dread* (W. W. Norton, 2003).

"I don't really read erotic literature as such. However, I very much enjoyed *Eye of the Beholder* by Marc Behm, which is described in a *New York Times* review as a 'private eye crime novel and psychological suspense story.' The eroticism came from the main character's obsession with a woman he was watching and how he came actually to identify with her in the end. I found it appealing that someone could abandon all sense of self in the service of someone else. It seemed both mad and inspired and, I believe, reminded me of the artistic impulse."

Conrad Aiken (1889–1973). When the Savannah-born Aiken was eleven, he discovered the bodies of his parents: His physician father had killed the boy's mother and then himself. At Harvard, Aiken made a lifelong friend in T. S. Eliot, whom he nicknamed "tse-tse," and in 1924 he edited Emily Dickinson's *Selected Poems,* which did much to establish her reputation. Exemplifying Aiken's strengths, "Sea Holly" takes its place in a tradition of landscape poems in which the natural world in its motions and gyrations seems to correspond to the human body. The "meeting of rock with rock, / The mating of rock and rock" is charged with erotic force not (or not just) because "rock" stands metaphorically for "breast" and the shape of a woman emerges from the side of the cliff, "virgin as rock," but because the waves break on the sand and the wind sprays the air with a fury and in a rhythm suggestive of carnal love.

Sandra Alcosser was born in Washington, D.C., in 1944. Her most recent book is *The Blue Vein*, 2006 (*livre d'artiste*, Brighton Press).

"Absolutely unmixed attention is *prayer*, wrote Simone Weil. Eros is absolutely unmixed attention: Loren Eisley's white wings moving inside a Manhattan evening; Colette's mother's house; Carl Philips's *Cortege*; Henri Cole's elephant in *Middle Earth*; Severo Sarduy's *Written on the Body*; Michael Ondaatje's dog paw. Jean Rhys: 'The earth was like a magnet which pulled me and sometimes I came near it, this identification or annihilation that I longed for.' Paul Shepherd: 'hairlessness developed with the increased sensuousness of human body surface.' George Seferis: 'The sea, the mountains that dance motionless; I found them the same in these rippled chitons: water turned into marble around the chests and the sides of headless fragments. I know my whole life won't be long enough to express what I have been trying to say for so many days now: this union of nature with a simple human body, this worthless thing.'"

Elizabeth Alexander was born in New York City in 1962. Her most recent book of poems is *American Sublime* (Graywolf, 2005).

"When I was the age of the speaker in the poem, the most important erotic writing to me was certainly Pablo Neruda's *Veinte Poemas de Amor y una Canción Desesperada*, with 'Every Day You Play with the Light of the Universe' being the anthem of a dreamed-of erotic life. I was also very taken with 1970s feminist novels starring sexually emancipated heroines: Rita Mae Brown's *Rubyfruit Jungle*, Erica Jong's *Fear of Flying*, Marilyn French's *The Women's Room*, and a bit later, Audre Lorde's 'biomythography,' *Zami*."

A. R. Ammons (1926–2001). Born in North Carolina, Archie Randolph Ammons taught for many years at Cornell University. A maverick talent, grandly ambitious yet capable of whimsy, he understood modern science and brought it to bear in chronicling his encounters with the natural world. Though committed to the particular, Ammons in a philosophical mood can speak about abstractions as though they were living organisms observing rituals of unity and linkage. "The sexual basis of all things rare is really apparent" is the first line of his book-length poem *Sphere*. "Their Sex Life" is a model of elegance, symmetry, economy, and wit; the word *failure* can refer to a person or an event, and the placement of *top* invites us to interpret the two lines as corresponding to a pair of human bodies.

Nin Andrews was born in Charlottesville, Virginia, in 1958. Her most recent book is *Sleeping with Houdini* (BOA Editions, 2007).
    Andrews writes:

> My favorite erotic poet is Vallejo
> who isn't exactly erotic but always makes me swoon
>
> with his two most famous poems,
> "Agape" and "*Piedra Negra Sobre Una Piedra Blanca.*"
>
> It's that quality of longing that poets have
> way too much of,
> and their terrible loneliness
> that would like to say
> as Vallejo does:
>
> "I would come to my door,
> I would shout to everyone,
> if you are missing anything, here it is!"
>
> And I'd love to.
> Yes, I'd love to go to his door
> and make love to him,
> perhaps on a Thursday in Paris
> on a day of heavy showers . . .
> I'd keep everyone from beating him,
> those whom he has done nothing to,
> (Why does the world want to beat our famous poets?)
>
> my Vallejo, yes, my own Vallejo
> who lives deep inside me now
> where he is safe at last,
> though he of course knows nothing about this . . .

Sarah Arvio was born in Philadelphia in 1954. Her most recent book is *Sono* (Knopf, 2006).

"A few years after writing 'Mirrors,' I happened to reread some poems by John Donne—and there, in 'A Valediction: Forbidding Mourning,' I found an odd word that had slipped into my poem: *sublunary*. Donne's argument: Only dull sublunary (earthbound) lovers care about 'eyes, lips, hands.' Refined lovers don't care if the bodies of their lovers have died: They have their intertwined souls! In 'Mirrors,' the opposite occurs. The speakers—who are souls—look back with longing and regret at the embodied life. Note that my list of 'breasts, balls, and lips' mirrors Donne's. I can't help feeling that his three sexy words ('eyes, lips, hands') betray a touch of irony."

W. H. Auden (1907–1973). Born in "old" York (England), Auden wrote "The Platonic Blow, by Miss Oral"—also known as "A Day for a Lay"—in New York in December 1948. By *Platonic* Auden meant *ideal,* not *nonphysical.* "Deciding that there ought to be one in the Auden Corpus, I am writing a purely pornographic poem," he told his companion Chester Kallman. "You should do a complementary one on the other major act." Auden later disavowed "The Platonic Blow," never including it among his works or admitting his authorship. Typescript copies circulated among gay friends and admirers, and in 1965 Ed Sanders of the rock group the Fugs released a print version. A pamphlet consisting of "The Platonic Blow" and the three-line poem "My Epitaph" appeared from Orchises Press in 1985. (The editor's note asserts that "The Platonic Blow," which was "never acknowledged by Auden, can hardly be copyrighted by his estate; moreover, it has previously appeared in so many unreliable editions that any claim to copyright must by this point have been compromised.") In the same year he wrote "The Platonic Blow," Auden made the observation that "All American writing gives the impression that Americans don't really care for girls at all. What the American man really wants is two things: he wants to be blown by a stranger while reading a newspaper, [and] he wants to be fucked by his buddy when he's drunk."

Ellen Bass was born in Philadelphia in 1947. Her most recent book of poems is *The Human Line* (Copper Canyon Press, 2007).
"Sharon Olds celebrates the power of the erotic: its intensity, wonder, intimacy, and joy so strong it borders on the frightening. It would be hard to choose one favorite, but some that come immediately to mind are 'Greed and Aggression,' 'Ecstasy,' 'Still Life,' 'Sex

Without Love,' and 'Celibacy at Twenty.' The imagination and precision of these poems is stunning. In a time when we're bombarded by sexual images that are detached and devoid of meaning, these poems show us sexual desire that is rooted in connection, passion, and amazement."

Ted Berrigan (1934–1983). Born in Providence, Rhode Island, Berrigan went to Catholic schools, joined the electrical workers' union before he joined the army, and came to New York City after studying literature at the University of Tulsa on the GI Bill. He had read Frank O'Hara and wanted to emulate the urban ways of his hero. In 1963 Berrigan wrote *The Sonnets*, his masterwork, in which he subjects the typical contents of a sonnet sequence to experimental methods; he would scramble lines, or repeat them, or lift them from other sources. Berrigan founded and edited *C* magazine, collaborated with painters and with other poets, and was a familiar presence at poetry events at St. Mark's Church in the East Village, which he helped make the semiofficial headquarters of a second generation of New York School poets. His work remains a vital influence on younger poets.

Elizabeth Bishop (1911–1979). Bishop was a poet of reticence and understatement who disliked the confessional mode and opposed the subordination of poetry to politics or feminism. She wrote little and published less, but her work is of the highest quality, and the poets of her own and succeeding generations have held her with a special affection. Born in Worcester, Massachusetts, Bishop went to Vassar College and was the model for a character in Mary McCarthy's Vassar-centric novel, *The Group*. On the week of her death, the last assignment Bishop gave to her MIT students was to read all of Theodore Roethke's poems in *The Norton Anthology* and to attempt a ballad, at least eight stanzas long, rhyming either A-B-C-B or A-B-A-B. "It is Marvellous. . ." first appeared in *The American Poetry Review,* was reprinted in *The Best American Poetry 1989,* and has, as Helen Vendler notes, "been accepted informally into the Bishop canon."

Star Black was born in Coronado, California, in 1946. Her recent books include *Ghostwood* and *Balefire.* A collection of her collages and Bill Knott's poems appeared under the title *Stigmata Errata Etcetera* from Saturnalia Books in 2007.

"I have always thought that if I were in a state of erotic blissfulness the last thing that I would want to do would be to write a poem; but, when banished to the literary sidelines, the consolation zone of memory or longing for what could always be remembered, I turn to the beckoning doors in the beautiful Song of Solomon, or Penelope's low-burning fire ('She wanted nothing he could not bring her by coming alone. / She wanted no fetchings. His arms would be her necklace') in Wallace Stevens's 'The World as Meditation,' or these lines from an early Donald Justice poem, 'Portraits of the Sixties' (1973): 'Pull down the shades. / Your black boyfriend is coming. / He's not like you. He wants / To live in the suburbs. / You want to paint.'"

Paul Blackburn (1926–1971). A Vermont native, Blackburn became a mentor to younger poets in New York City in the 1960s. In a memoir, Martha King likened Blackburn to a kind of divine eavesdropper, watching from the sidelines, whether "sitting on the subway, or looking out of a luncheonette window. Blackburn documenting the exact particulars of discarded newspapers and empty wine bottles around the base of a statue. Or of a woman's clothing and precisely what it reveals of her body underneath, and who else on the street is also noticing."

Robin Blaser was born in Denver, Colorado, in 1925. His most recent books are *The Holy Forest: Collected Poems* and *The Fire: Collected Essays*, both published by the University of California Press in 2006.

"At eighty-two I find everything erotic—that's the stomping ground of all intelligence—the intellect picks it up from the ground and gives language as a kind of music to dance around."

George Henry Boker (1823–1890). Boker was born in Philadephia, the son of a prominent banker. During the Civil War, he raised funds in support of the Union war effort. In 1871 President Grant appointed him U.S. minister to Turkey, and he later served with distinction as envoy extraordinary and minister plenipotentiary to Russia. Boker wrote plays, of which the most celebrated was *Francesca da Rimini*, a version of the Paolo and Francesca story familiar to readers of Dante's *Inferno*. All but 76 of Boker's 389 sonnets form a massive "sequence on profane love," in which he contemplates the tyranny of passion and recalls the "wicked hours" passed in youth with "wanton

Circe and her bestial kin." The sonnet here, like most in the sequence, went unpublished in Boker's lifetime.

Catherine Bowman was born in El Paso, Texas, in 1957. Her most recent books are *Notarikon* (2006) and *The Plath Cabinet* (2008), both from Four Way Books.

"One of my favorite works of erotic writing is Georges Bataille's *Story of the Eye*, because it's beautiful, strange, and so dirty."

Charles Bukowski (1920–1994). Born in Andernach, Germany, the only child of an American soldier and a German mother, Bukowski grew up in Los Angeles, attended Los Angeles City College from 1939 to 1941, then left school and moved to New York City to become a writer. He gave up writing in favor of drinking in 1946. After he developed a bleeding ulcer, he decided to take up writing again. He worked at a variety of blue-collar jobs to support his writing, including mail carrier and postal clerk, dishwasher, guard, elevator operator, gas station attendant, stock boy, warehouse worker, and shipping clerk. But he never worked in academe, and he wrote with disdain of the Beats and others ("hucksters of the / despoiled word") who issue rebellious proclamations from "sad university / lecterns." Bukowski felt that, as the hero of his own life, he had the right to make up the details of his stories, which he told with such conviction and authenticity that readers took them as unvarnished truth. He identified his natural constituency as "the defeated, the demented, and the damned."

Robert Olen Butler was born in Granite City, Illinois, in 1945. *Intercourse* was published by Chronicle Books in 2008. Butler's prose poem included in *The Best American Erotic Poems* is one of sixty-two that he collected in his book *Severance* (2006). Each entry contains exactly 240 words and records the last thoughts in the mind of a man or woman who has been beheaded. The working assumption is that after decapitation the brain continues to function for ninety seconds, and that in a heightened state of emotion people speak at the rate of 160 words per minute.

"My favorite work of erotic writing—not in its ability to arouse sexual desire but as an expression of crazy wonderful erotic fervor—is the Song of Solomon (King James Version, of course). I love, in this case, to pretend that the biblical literalists of the world, who feel

God's own personal voice speaking through every word of the Bible, are right. Oh my. How God loves sex and how goofily over-the-top He is about it. For example, 'Thy teeth are as a flock of sheep which go up from the washing, whereof every one beareth twins and there is not one barren among them.' And 'Thy belly is like a heap of wheat set about with lilies.' The Man's usually sublime, universe-building voice ('in the beginning was the Word') has gone wildly out of metaphorical tune and, in doing so, betrays a love of the body, of sex, of sensuality that is very endearing. And when He says, 'the roof of thy mouth [is] like the best wine for my beloved, that goeth down sweetly,' I say unto you the Scripture-driven sodomy laws are dead wrong. The blow job has a clear sanction in the literal truth of the Holy Bible."

Hayden Carruth was born in Waterbury, Connecticut, in 1921. His books include *Collected Shorter Poems, 1946–1991* and *Collected Longer Poems* (1994), both from Copper Canyon Press.

"My choice of a favorite erotic poem from recent American literature is Galway Kinnell's 'Last Gods.'"

Editor's note: Kinnell's poem is included in *The Best American Erotic Poems* (see page 92).

Heather Christle was born in Wolfeboro, New Hampshire, in 1980.

"It is hard not to love Charles Simic's 'Breasts.'"

Editor's note: Simic's poem is included in *The Best American Erotic Poems* (see page 118).

Lucille Clifton was born in Depew, New York, in 1936. Her *Blessing the Boats: New and Selected Poems 1988–2000* (BOA Editions, 2000) won the National Book Award.

"Among my favorite erotic works are those of Richard Shelton, a contemporary poet in Arizona:

> I touch you
> like a blind man
> touches the dice
> and finds he has won.

Also E. E. Cummings: 'somewhere i have never traveled gladly,beyond.'"

Marc Cohen was born in Brooklyn, New York, in 1951. His latest book of poems is *Opening the Window* (Sheep Meadow Press, 2005).

"My favorite piece of erotic literature, 'The Deserts of Love,' is also the first prose poem that Arthur Rimbaud wrote; he was seventeen years old at the time and had just read Baudelaire's collection of prose poems, *Paris Spleen.* Louise Varèse, the original translator of the poem, called it 'pure poetry,' and I'll take that judgment one step further and call it pure erotic poetry. I've always admired the poem because it captures the self-discovery and romance of the erotic as well as the despair that follows when the flowers of ecstasy wilt and die. The poem renders two dreams by a narrator who is in the grips of the psyche's unconscious longing to engage in sexual love. The narrator is probably aware of what Baudelaire wrote in his *Intimate Journals*: 'That which is created in the Mind is more living than Matter,' and can at least take heart if not comfort from the maxim."

Billy Collins was born in New York City in 1941. His books include *The Trouble with Poetry and Other Poems* (Random House, 2005).

"So much erotica, so little time. But if I had to pick two, I would include the Victorian classic *The Whippingham Papers* (1888), which, as the title implies, is a collection of stories and poems featuring flagellation. Algernon Charles Swinburne contributes some verses. One consoling feature of such tales is the presentation of a society containing just the right balance of sadists and masochists, an answer to the common complaint that in real life the latter grossly outnumber the former. More backsides than whips.

"A close second would be Nicholson Baker's *The Fermata,* the story of an office temp named Arno Strine, who has actually figured out how to stop time and who exercises this amazing supernatural power by taking off women's clothes while he has them on Pause."

Dennis Cooper was born in Pasadena, California, in 1953, and grew up in the Southern California cities of Covina and Arcadia. His books include *The Sluts,* a novel (Carroll & Graf, 2005).

Hart Crane (1899–1932). Born in Garretsville, Ohio, the son of the candy manufacturer who invented LifeSavers, Crane resembles an American Keats: He wrote great letters, had the loftiest literary aspirations, and died too young. A factory accident at the Crane company in Cleveland provoked Crane to write "Episode of Hands" in 1920. He settled in New York in 1924 and lived for a time in Columbia Heights in Brooklyn, where he commenced work on his most ambitious poem. "Only later did Crane learn that the house where the vision of *The Bridge* first came to him, and where he finished it, had been the property of Washington Roebling, the paralyzed engineer of the Brooklyn Bridge, and that the very room where Crane lived and wrote had been used by Roebling as an observation tower to watch the bridge's construction" (Waldo Frank). In a letter, Crane described the epiphany he'd had when under the influence of "aether and amnesia" in the dentist's chair: "Something like an objective voice kept saying to me—'You have the higher consciousness—you have the higher consciousness. This is something that very few have. This is what is called genius.'" Crane would drink to excess, play a Spanish bolero on his Victrola, and compose. He had a liking for sailors and rough trade. Beaten up in the early-morning hours of April 27, 1932, he jumped to his death at noon that day off the deck of the *Orizaba,* returning to the United States from Mexico.

Laura Cronk was born in New Castle, Indiana, in 1977.

"Vladimir Mayakovsky sent the poem 'Letter from Paris to Comrade Kostrov on the Nature of Love' to his editor instead of the political poems he had been commissioned to write. This may have been maddening for Kostrov's superiors, but it was a wonderfully subversive and sexy thing to do for poetry. It's the kind of stunt that can secure a poet a place as a literary heartthrob. I love that Mayakovsky's poems, this one included, embody toughness along with tenderness, coarseness along with delicacy. These lines are among my favorites:

> To love
>> means this:
>>> to run
>> into the depths of a yard
>>>> and, till the rook-black night,
>> chop wood
>>> with a shining axe,
>> giving full play
>>> to one's
>>>> strength."

E. E. Cummings (1894–1962). The Harvard-educated Cummings takes typographic liberties and eschews the uppercase in his poems, concealing a romantic soul beneath an experimental veneer. He rejoices in lust, spring, the "sweet spontaneous earth," and the breasts of a woman in love ("two sharp delightful strutting towers"). In a "nonlecture" he gave at his alma mater, he called himself a "burlesk addict of long standing (who has many times worshipped at the shrine of progressive corporeal revelation)." Cummings's deviations from conventional grammar and punctuation permit him to achieve at times a kind of abstract lyricism. In the spaces between the words and lines as much as in the content, he enacts the quickening of the heart—"my somewhereallover me heart my"—that accompanies arousal. Cummings died in 1962 in New Hampshire. He had just finished chopping wood.

James Cummins was born in Columbus, Ohio, in 1948. His most recent book is *Then and Now* (Swallow Press, 2004).

"First might not be best but might be most powerful. In Indianapolis, in the seventh grade, Mike Mauro, a friend of mine who was a couple of years older and the brother of my first love, Maria, tried to teach me how to masturbate. The first part of this ritual entailed biking over to Cossell's drugstore and 'hocking' (shoplifting) two sexy paperbacks to help get us into the mood. I forget the title of Mike's, but it did the trick later in the evening; my own was *The Bachelor's Guide to Women*, which didn't. My family soon moved out of the neighborhood—there was a rumor that a black family had bought a house a few blocks away—and I lost touch with Mike and, more sadly, Maria. But a mere few months later, in a different drugstore on Shadeland Boulevard, I hocked another book, *And When She Was Bad*, about a nymphomaniac named Ellie Dannon and her unsuspecting husband, Dick Sterling, and soon found the bliss (and compulsive behavior patterns) Mike had promised. Ellie had some sort of something pressing on some sort of gland that caused her to need to have sex with anyone who put his hands on her breasts. Finally, I thought, after all those years in Catholic schools—a sign God might actually exist! Even as I stood in the drugstore aisle, reading avidly, I knew I'd said good-bye to the land of *The Bachelor's Guide to Women* forever."

J. V. Cunningham (1911–1985). A proponent of the plain style, Cunningham (born in Cumberland, Maryland) studied with Yvor

Winters at Stanford University and resisted modernism even more strenuously than Winters did. A brilliant epigrammatist in the manner of Martial, whom he translated from the Latin, Cunningham wrote with wit, concision, and sometimes ribaldry. Robert Lowell, among others, felt that Cunningham was the "greatest modern master of the comma." The classical nature of his enterprise clashes fruitfully with the totally American and anti-classical subjects he brought into his poetry, such as the deleted expletives in transcripts of Richard Nixon's Watergate tapes or the distractions at a Las Vegas casino.

Olena Kalytiak Davis was born in Detroit, Michigan, in 1963. Her most recent book is *Shattered Sonnets Love Cards and Other Off and Back Handed Importunities* (Tin House/Bloomsbury, 2003).

"Sure, I've had nightstand copies of *Delta of Venus* and *The Story of O,* but mostly (or perhaps momentarily), it seems my reading has been unbelievably chaste. Nabokov and Steve Almond, I guess. A couple pretty good e-mails."

Emily Dickinson (1830–1886). Among our greatest poets, the reclusive "Belle of Amherst" was unknown in her lifetime and died without an inkling of her posthumous fame. Dickinson derived her homemade stanza form from the church hymnal; she fashioned her own audacious system of punctuation centering on the dash. Telling the truth but telling it slant, her poems communicate sensual pleasure, ecstatic release, "solemn nameless need," and a terrifying but longed-for violent consummation: "One—imperial—Thunderbolt— / That scalps your naked Soul—." When Bernini in his marble *Ecstasy of St. Theresa* uses erotic means to advance a religious theme, or when John Donne does the same in his *Holy Sonnets,* the spectator or reader may conflate the spiritual pretext and the sexual metaphor. In Emily Dickinson's poems, the imperatives of Eros and those of a personally conceived heaven exist in a yet more complicated relation. Dickinson attended Mount Holyoke Female Seminary at a time of rampant Christian revivalism. She resisted the pressure to convert, doubting not the existence of God but the obligation to submit to him. In her poems, she wrestles with the deity to such an extent that a scholar may contend, as Cynthia Griffin Wolfe does, that Jacob's wrestling match with the angel of the Lord in Genesis serves as Dickinson's biblical archetype. A reading of the poem beginning "In Winter in my Room" may illustrate Freud's program of dream interpretation on the one hand and his theory of the uncanny on the other.

Stephen Dobyns was born in Orange, New Jersey, in 1941. His most recent book is *Mystery, So Long* (Penguin, 2005).

"There is a novel entitled *The Two Deaths of Señora Puccini* (1988), which is the best depiction of sexual obsession, in fiction, that I know."

Nicholas Roeg adapted Dobyns's novel in his 1994 movie, *Two Deaths*.

Mark Doty was born in Maryville, Tennessee, in 1953. His most recent book is *Dog Years* (HarperCollins, 2007).

"There are contemporary erotic poems I love—by James L. White, Allen Ginsberg, and Thom Gunn—but I have to name Whitman's 'Song of Myself' as the one favorite I'd never want to be without. For its expansive, generous love of the speaker's body and bodies in general, and for its astonishingly forthright and sometimes weird moments: the soul giving the self a blow job; the sky sending forth 'libidinous prongs'; the singer aroused by the night ('Press close barebosomed night! . . . Mad naked summer night!'). Whitman blurs his pronouns and the subjects he's addressing until all of creation seems sexually charged, the world a grand congress of sexual forces, even the wind, 'whose soft-tickling genitals rub against me . . .' Whitman's great outpouring is so exuberantly horny that it can't stop at the body of any single beloved, but must move out and out, encompassing more and more in the circumference of desiring, and thus sexuality slips right into the realm of the soul."

Denise Duhamel was born in Providence, Rhode Island, in 1961. Her most recent book is *Two and Two* (University of Pittsburgh Press, 2005).

"My favorite erotic poem is E. E. Cummings's 'i like my body when it is with your,' which is playful and mysterious in such passages as this:

> . . . slowly stroking the, shocking fuzz
> of your electric fur, and what-is-it comes
> over parting flesh . . .

"The pubic hair in the poem becomes part animal, part lightning; the 'what-is-it' underneath is divine, that for which there is no poetic name. In a poem that is both sexy and tender, E. E. Cummings describes the beloved's eyes as 'big Love-crumbs.'"

Robert Duncan (1919–1988). An avowed homosexual at a time when such an admission ran the risk of literary rejection, Duncan (born in Oakland, California) was educated at Berkeley. He taught at Black Mountain College and is often considered in the company of Charles Olson and Robert Creeley. Duncan became a respected figure in the San Francisco Renaissance. Of "The Torso," Gregory Woods has written that the poem's "shifting focus corresponds with that of a man kneeling to fellate his lover: the collar bone, chest, navel, and pubic hair are examined in turn. But the occasion of the poem involves the two men in reversed roles. While the speaker's mind moves down the torso of the lover, the lover himself is on his knees, fellating the speaker. The fantasy of the one duplicates the deeds of the other."

Russell Edson was born in Connecticut in 1935. His recent books are *The Rooster's Wife* (Boa Editions, Ltd., 2005) and *En Afton På Grisarnas Teater* (Karneval förlag, Stockholm, 2007).

"Of all my readings in erotica, the most erotic has come from the pens of various science writers who have described the primal sensual event called the 'big bang.'"

Lynn Emanuel was born in Mount Kisco, New York, in 1949. Her most recent book is *Then, Suddenly* (University of Pittsburgh, 1999).

"My favorite piece of erotic literature is the *Sleeping Beauty* trilogy by Anne Rice writing under the name A. N. Roquelaure. The novels, published between 1983 and 1985 and still in print, are, as Rice describes them, 'novels of discipline and surrender.' Over the course of the books, the heroine, Beauty, is awakened and punished—for being beautiful. In her erotic slavery, Beauty becomes completely objectified, and as she becomes less and less herself/a self, the power of her masters and punishers to inflict suffering upon her is erased. The trilogy composes a meditation on the ways in which the vanquished can and do seize power. This is a thinking person's eroticism."

Janice Erlbaum was born in New York City in 1969. Her latest book is *Have You Found Her* (Villard, 2008).

"My favorite work of erotic writing is a short memoir by Honey Bruce, wife of Lenny, originally published in a late-1970s issue of

Playboy magazine I found when I was nine. She loved her husband pretty hard. The whole issue was good, as I recall—it made me want to become either a Bunny, a stripper, or a junkie comedian."

Jill Alexander Essbaum was born in Bay City, Texas, in 1971. Her new book is *Harlot* (No Tell Books, 2007).

"Must I pick just one? I've memories of a schoolgirl self as she riffles through doggedly dog-eared pages of Harold Robbins novels, scanning for sentences that *steam*. Or in junior high, the thumbing, strumming me raptly wrapped up in the vulgar divulgences of a certain *Secret Garden* (er, that's Nancy Friday's and *not* Frances Hodgson Burnett's). But for the pearly pinks of greatest price, my warring Puritanical/Prurient selves must always and evermore return to the (*oh so very*) Good Book. A voluptuous buffet of bawd! Care to fellate? 'And his fruit is sweet to my taste' (Song of Solomon 2:3). Desirous of down-going? 'Come . . . blow upon my garden, that the spices thereof may flow out' (Song of Solomon 4:16). How about a straight-up lay? 'And I went unto the prophetess' (Isaiah 8:3). Feeling indiscriminate? Tomcattish? 'Thou hast played the harlot with many lovers' (Jeremiah 3:1). On and on it goes (*and under and on top of and from behind . . .*). But for my favorite perverse verse, I'm keen to point to one that—were I equally inclined and indecorous—I might assign to particularize my own prickly proclivities: 'There she lusted after her lovers, whose genitals were like those of donkeys and whose emission was like that of horses' (Ezekiel 23:20). Preach it, sister!"

Jenny Factor was born in New Haven, Connecticut, in 1969. Her book *Unraveling at the Name* appeared from Copper Canyon Press in 2002.

"I was once hopelessly in love with an entirely unavailable woman. While she expressed no passion toward me, she would from time to time hand me poetry she thought I would like. Like all frustrated lovers, I took these little tokens deep into my own breath. One such donation was Marilyn Hacker's *Love, Death, and the Changing of the Seasons*—a sonnet collection that transformed the rest of my life. Marilyn Hacker's verse novel tells of a doomed love affair between a student and a teacher. The semantic sizzle is astonishing. 'Age is not the muddle of the matter,' Hacker writes. And she ingeniously rhymes 'geste héroïque' to 'a fit of pique.' (Incidentally, I later discovered Hacker's tonal twin in John Berryman's *Sonnets, 1967*— another sexy little volume.) But it was the seventeenth sonnet in the collection that delivered the major blow. Hacker writes: 'First, I want to make you come with my hand / While I watch you and kiss you, and *if you cry*' (emphasis added). I blinked. Imagine a woman being moved to tears like that! I kept the page open on the bedstand overnight. Was there more to this sex thing than I had thought? I closed the book and bit hard into Eve's apple."

Alan Feldman was born in Far Rockaway, New York, in 1945. His most recent book is *A Sail to Great Island* (University of Wisconsin Press, 2004).

"Tough to choose a favorite. In English literature, I remember having a serious crush on Chaucer's Criseyde. I found the middle stanza of Sir Thomas Wyatt's 'They Flee from Me' very sexy and empathized with his feeling of love slipping through his fingers. But among Americans? So much in Whitman and Dickinson: Section 11 in 'Song of Myself' re the twenty-ninth bather; Dickinson's 'Wild Nights—Wild Nights!' I've always loved Prufrock's neurotic, erotic love song, and Pound's 'The River Merchant's Wife,' so understated and heartbreaking: 'I desired my dust to be mingled with yours / Forever and forever and forever. / Why should I climb the look out?' William Carlos Williams was such a lusty admirer of well-formed women, as in his 'The Young Housewife,' though my favorite is 'Danse Russe,' in which he's attracted to himself! I greatly admire Bishop's villanelle 'One Art,' which, I take it, is about the loss of a dear love (to suicide?). And Frank O'Hara's whole series of love poems to the dancer Vincent Warren, tracing the arc of their affair; 'Joe's Jacket' and 'Steps' would be just two of my favorites. And Kenneth Koch's goofy, funny, and infectiously joyous 'To You,' which begins 'I love you as a sheriff searches for a walnut / That will solve a murder case unsolved for years.' Robert Creeley's 'The Warning': 'For love—I would / split open your head and put / a candle in / behind the eyes.' And Alan Dugan's anguished self-crucifixion in 'Love Song, I and Thou.' More recently, I've been impressed by the way Sharon Olds gets sex, along with all its ferocity and bodily fluids, into poems like 'Greed and Aggression.' In prose, I've always enjoyed Updike's description of women's bodies, beginning as early as 'A & P,' with its two scoops of vanilla ice cream."

Editor's note: Emily Dickinson's "Wild Nights—Wild Nights!" is included in *The Best American Erotic Poems* (see page 13).

Beth Ann Fennelly was born in Rahway, New Jersey, in 1971. Her latest book is *Unmentionables* (W. W. Norton, 2008).

"Twenty years ago, there was a zoo in the Czech Republic that lost its funding and fell on hard times. Several cages became so decrepit that animals of different species were combined. A young peacock was put in a tortoise's cage, and because the peacock was nearing sexual maturity, it imprinted on the tortoise. Wherever the tortoise lumbered to, the peacock followed, shrieking and shimmying its fan of iridescent feathers in a display both comic and tragic.

"I suppose such adolescent imprinting is to blame for my spectacularly bad taste in erotica; I confess that the sexiest thing I've ever read is *Flowers in the Attic* by V. C. Andrews. I was in sixth grade. I'd heard older girls talking about the book, and I checked it out of the library, although my parents had forbidden it. I used to sneak it into the bathroom and read it in the tub. Filled with violence, incest, a wicked grandmother, and a deep, dark attic, it spoke to me on some über-Freudian level.

"Much like the peacock's, my passion was doomed. One day while I was reading in the bath, my mother walked in, so I drowned the book under the bubbles to avoid detection. After she left, I dried it with my sister's hairdryer and tried to return it in the library book drop, but the pages were swollen and wavy. The librarian made me pay forty hard-earned babysitting dollars for a new copy, and I was too embarrassed to check it out again. Perhaps it's just as well I've never reread it as an adult. I'm sure it's atrociously written. I seem to remember a lot of exclamation marks. Let it fester in the attic of my imagination, where the roots of those flowers have merely grown deeper with the passage of time."

Bob Flanagan (1952–1996). Born in New York City, Flanagan grew up in Glendora, California, a suburb of Los Angeles. The obituary that appeared in *The New York Times* on January 6, 1996, described him as a "former cystic fibrosis poster boy" who became a poet and performance artist. Ordinarily, victims of the disease do not reach adulthood, and Flanagan was said to have been one of the ailment's longest-living survivors. "He attributed his longevity in part to his ability to 'fight pain with pain,' by which he meant that he took control of his suffering through the ritualized pain of sado-masochism" in his performance art, wrote Roberta Smith.

Robert Frost (1874–1963). Although Frost wrote "The Subverted Flower" early enough to have included it in his first book, *A Boy's Will* (1913), his wife, Elinor, forbade him to publish it in her lifetime, perhaps because it is based on an unfortunate episode in their courtship. The poem appeared in the 1942 collection *A Witness Tree* when its author was sixty-seven. Randall Jarrell described "The Subverted Flower" as "sinister, condemning, tender." Frost himself claimed that the poem concerned frigidity in women, and it is extraordinary how many able commentators either fail to challenge this claim or evade discussion of the poem. It is likely that the flower is allegorically the boy's penis, and his actions ("A hand hung like a paw, / An arm worked like a saw") suggest the "shame" of masturbation or of coerced oral sex interrupted only by the arrival of the girl's mother. Is the "foam" at the end of the poem evidence? What does the sustained animal imagery signify? The puzzles of "The Subverted Flower" will take more than one reading to solve.

Isabella Stewart Gardner (1915–1981). Isabella Stewart Gardner was the great-grandniece of the founder of the museum in Boston that bears her name. "The Milkman" was published in *Poetry* magazine in 1952 and in her first book, *Birthdays from the Ocean,* in 1955. Her poems reflect the influence of Martin Buber's "I-Thou" philosophy on the one hand and the rich sonority of Dylan Thomas's poems on the other. Her pleasure in the opposite sex is palpable: "How struts my love my cavalier / How crows he like a chanticleer / How softly am I spurred my dear; / Our bed is feathered with desire / And this yard safe from fox and fire."

Amy Gerstler was born in San Diego, California, in 1956. Her most recent book of poems is *Ghost Girl* (Penguin, 2004).

"The first book I encountered that focused on sex was the two-volume set of *The Psychology of Sex* by Havelock Ellis. My parents had a battered copy of this tome, and around age nine, I noticed it in our family room on a very high shelf just under the ceiling. As I was on the hunt for books with sexual content, finding this one was like hitting a gusher. I made a project of dipping into *The Psychology of Sex* whenever my parents went out. This involved climbing up on a cabinet in order to pull the heavy books from their perch, and then sitting atop the cabinet to read, so that when I heard my parents at the door, I could quickly replace the books on the shelf, get down, run to my room, and simulate being a model citizen. These books were not, I now realize, intended as erotic literature, but they were among the first books that served that purpose for me, and therefore I am fond of them. They have a place of honor in the office I write in today. They were my introduction to how exciting science could be. I liked the old-fashioned practice of giving the names of sexual acts in Latin (which gave me many hours of excited puzzlement as I tried to decipher, via context, what these key words might mean), not to mention the sexual case studies and anecdotes, the fascinating cavalcade of human activities and longings considered 'aberrant,' and the delicious practice of sneakily reading something deemed forbidden. There was a long section on the erotics of modesty that influenced me deeply. A few months after I discovered *The Psychology of Sex,* I noticed on another part of that lofty shelf a paperback copy (also rather tattered) of a novel called *Lolita.* I'd heard this was a racy book, so I tried to read it. My memory of this first reading of Nabokov's masterpiece is dim, though I do remember finding a lot of it confusing. There was an image of Humbert staring worshipfully at one of Lolita's pubic hairs in a dry bathtub, and he compared it to a question mark. This image electrified me, and I have never forgotten it."

Allen Ginsberg (1926–1997). No one writing the cultural history of our age can omit the poet of "Howl" and "Kaddish," psychic phantasmagoria and Jewish sorrow. Ginsberg was the quintessential Beat poet, an "angelheaded hipster" who braved ostracism and censure for the sake of his unabashedly "queer" vision of life, death, drugs, America, and the higher consciousness. The most poignant line in "Wichita Vortex Sutra" (1966), which Ginsberg wrote at the height of the war in Vietnam, is "I here declare the end of the War!" The poem did not stop the bombings, withdraw the troops, hound a president from office, restore unity and purpose to a divided populace, or bring peace to Southeast Asia. No, Ginsberg had beaten in the void his luminous wings in vain. But the test of a prophecy does not rest in its instant fulfillment, and Ginsberg was a prophet. "Preaching and colonizing a brave new never-never world of bearded, beaded, marijuana-smoking, mantra-chanting euphoria, Ginberg set the style for the Be-Ins, Love-Ins, Kiss-Ins, Chant-Ins, sacred orgies, and demon-dispelling circumambulations of local draft boards," Jane Kramer wrote in 1968.

Dana Gioia was born in Los Angeles in 1950. "Alley Cat Love Song" appeared in his book *Interrogations at Noon* (2001).

"Eros is such a universal theme in literature that to choose a favorite work is an exercise in sublimation. Selecting one masterpiece is to renounce all of the other enticing works, so let me indulge in literary bigamy. I consider Stendhal's *The Charterhouse of Parma* the most profound study of romantic and sexual love ever written, but its Olympian status makes my praise seem like the most threadbare received opinion. Let me, therefore, laud a now neglected novel, Lawrence Durrell's *Justine*. The opening book of the *Alexandria Quartet, Justine* is a poet's novel—slightly overwritten, weirdly plotted, and deeply subjective—but let's not niggle. The book is also an idiosyncratic masterpiece—a feverish, brilliant, and unforgettable account of doomed (is there any other kind?) erotic obsession. Despite its faults, *Justine* will outlast any number of current prizewinning novels, because it explores, with a potent mixture of cruel candor and tender regret, the dark corners of the human heart."

Louise Glück was born in New York City in 1943. Her most recent book of poems is *Averno* (Farrar, Straus and Giroux, 2006).

"I can choose a poet—Cavafy—not a single poem. My own work learned immensely from his detachment and austerity and, in many of the poems, a strange slowing down of time: in Cavafy, an expression of fatedness and irrevocability—the poems exist in a space beyond choice or reason, beyond pleasure. In prose, I love *The Story of O* and Duras's *The Lover*."

Linda Gregg was born in Suffern, New York, in 1942. Her most recent book of poems is *In the Middle Distance* (Graywolf Press, 2006).

Gregg names the Song of Solomon (the Song of Songs) "to salvage it. To preserve the possibility of saving the erotic the way it was, long ago, at its best."

Beth Gylys was born in Passaic, New Jersey, in 1964. Her most recent book is *Spot in the Dark* (Silverfish Review Press, 2004).

"While hardly a traditional piece of erotica, Marguerite Duras's novel *L'Amant* (*The Lover*) transports me with its erotic vision. This exquisite novel-poem addresses the erotic as embodied in all physicality (not just human physicality) and as akin to and intensified by pain. I love the book for its brave, unflinching eye and its celebration of erotic pleasure and the way it can coexist with torment, rage, and despair."

Donald Hall was born in New Haven, Connecticut, in 1928. His most recent collection of poems is *White Apples and the Taste of Stone* (Houghton Mifflin, 2006).

"I don't really have a favorite erotic poem. For erotic writing, I would name the 'Penelope' section of *Ulysses*. I know that Joyce is writing in the voice of a woman, apparently aided by Nora Barnacle, but I find myself thoroughly convinced, and aroused."

Judith Hall was born in Washington, D.C., in 1951. Her most recent book of poems is *Three Trios*, translations of J II (TriQuarterly Books/Northwestern University Press, 2007).

"For someone introduced at too tender an age to *The Story of O* (1965), criticism, like Angela Carter's *Sadeian Woman and the Ideology of Pornography* (1979), offered predictable stimuli and stimuli as anodyne. Unpredictable erotica—reading that was not disciplined, isolated violence, not pitifully beyond the pale, but lively as life—came later, an acquired taste."

Robert Hass was born in San Francisco in 1941. His books include *Time and Materials: Poems 1997–2005* (Ecco) and *Now & Then: The Poet's Choice Columns, 1997–2000* (Shoemaker & Hoard).

"Trying to think of erotic poems that I admire, I thought first of Shakespeare's 'Venus and Adonis' and then of Anthony Burgess's imagination (in *Nothing Like the Sun*) of the poem's source in the relationship between the young Will Shakespeare and Anne Hathaway. Sexy poems: Herrick is sexy, especially 'Upon Julia's Clothes.' The whole of *A Midsummer Night's Dream* is sexy in one way, and *Antony and Cleopatra* is sexy in another. All of Donne's *Songs and Sonnets* are sexy, and the idea of Sappho's poems, though we have only two of them, is sexy, but it's hard to make a judgment about the poems themselves, and here we come to the fact that blurs the whole issue. Really gorgeous poems are sexy. So Hart Crane's 'To Brooklyn Bridge' is sexy in that way, and so is Donne's 'Good Friday, Riding Westward.' And for me it's often been the case that the poems of people I find sexy are deeply sexy. So leaving aside the fact that the most erotic poems are not necessarily poems with erotic subjects, but belong to the two categories of 1) amazing poems and 2) striking poems by people who are sexy to you, there are a few poems about desire or about sexuality that come to mind. The eleventh section of

'Song of Myself.' Dickinson's 'Wild Nights!' and her 'Come slowly—Eden!' D. H. Lawrence's 'Gloire de Dijon' is a sexy poem, a sort of verbal Renoir, and Michael Ondaatje's 'The Cinnamon Peeler' is a sexy poem. A lot of Gertrude Stein's *Lifting Belly* is quite delicious, and that might be a place to end this note:

> Kiss my lips. She did.
> Kiss my lips again she did.
> Kiss my lips over and over and over again she did.
> I have feathers.
> Gentle fishes.
> Do you think about apricots. We find them very beautiful. It is not alone their color it is their seeds that charm us. We find it a change.
> Lifting belly is so strange."

Editor's note: See page 26 for a longer excerpt from Stein's *Lifting Belly.* Emily Dickinson's "Come slowly—Eden!" and "Wild Nights—Wild Nights!" and are also included in *The Best American Erotic Poems* (see pages 12 and 13).

Terrance Hayes was born in Columbia, South Carolina, in 1971. His most recent book is *Wind in a Box* (Penguin, 2006).

"Lynda Hull's 'Black Mare' (in *The Collected Poems of Lynda Hull*) is a sort of doomed erotic poem. The speaker recalls a damaged love (full of drug use, desolate hotels, elevated trains, and winter), and all the blood of the poem is in Hull's intense lyricism, her hot, lush syntax. . . . For the erotic without the snow, I go to Neruda's love sonnets."

Tony Hoagland was born in Tucson, Arizona, in 1953. His latest book is *Real Sofistikashun: Essays on Craft and Poetry* (Graywolf Press, 2006).

"Some of the most erotic writing I know is found in Rilke's *Duino Elegies,* the famous 'Ninth' in particular, in which the poet queries, demands, praises, promises, and then swooningly consents to be entered completely by earth: 'Earth, isn't this what you want? An invisible re-arising in us? . . . What is your urgent command, if not transformation?' (trans. J. B. Leishman and Stephen Spender).

"The extended passage is unmistakably the address of ardent lover to beloved, and Rilke's athletic, tremulous syntax, in its swooping climaxes and surrenders, is thrillingly sexy in its brilliant performance of both masculine and feminine roles. Rilke reminds us how erotic the spiritual life can be, and his enactment of this encounter conjures up, for me, a moving, breathing body. It's hot stuff, and it always makes me want to pray harder."

Richard Howard was born in Cleveland, Ohio, in 1929. His most recent book of poems is *The Silent Treatment* (Turtle Point Press, 2005).

"No favorites, but liberators; Jean Genet's *Notre-Dame-des-Fleurs* revealed to this reader and writer the pleasures, the shames, and the ecstasies of the sexual person, the mental body—not only revealed but engraved in the memory or somewhere forever."

Langston Hughes (1902–1967). A leading figure of the Harlem Renaissance in the 1920s, Hughes was born in Joplin, Missouri, and began writing poetry as a teenager in Lincoln, Illinois. "We younger Negro artists who create now intend to express our individual dark-skinned selves without fear or shame," he wrote in 1926. "If white people are pleased we are glad. If they are not, it doesn't matter. We know we are beautiful. And ugly too. The tom-tom cries and the tom-tom laughs. If colored people are pleased we are glad. If they are not, their displeasure doesn't matter either." In such books as *The Weary Blues* (1926), his first collection, and *Montage of a Dream Deferred* (1951), Hughes derived the formal or rhythmic models for his poems from music—the blues and bebop jazz in particular. His taste ran the gamut from the baroque harpsichord to the singer Bessie Smith. As he wrote in "Theme for English B," a poem recollecting the year he spent as a student at Columbia ("this college on the hill above Harlem"), he liked getting "a pipe for a Christmas present, / or records—Bessie, bop, or Bach."

Cynthia Huntington was born in Meadville, Pennsylvania, in 1951. Her most recent book is *The Radiant* (Four Way Books, 2003).

"I choose *Forever Amber*, Kathleen Winsor's best-selling 1947 novel that was made into a movie with Linda Darnell. It's about the plague in London and a girl who slept her way through it with a diverse bunch of male partners. This is how Debs Meyer began his review of the novel in *Yank*, the U.S. Army newspaper: '*Forever*

Amber is the story of a girl laid in the 18th century.' Sex during the plague in London stays on my mind."

Denis Johnson was born in Munich, Germany, in 1949. His most recent book is *Tree of Smoke,* a novel (Farrar, Straus and Giroux, 2007).

"My favorite—probably the favorite of many—is Sir Thomas Wyatt's 'They Flee from Me.' It's simultaneously sad and moving and erotic. And full of truth about love."

Paul Jones was born in Hickory, North Carolina, in 1950. *What the Welsh and Chinese Have in Common* was published by North Carolina Writers Network in 1986.

"Dafydd ap Gwilym (c. 1315–c. 1370) is considered one of the greatest poets in the Welsh language. An innovator in style, range, and subject, he wrote religious verse, nature poems, praise poems, slapstick self-effacing tales of thwarted love, troubadour-influenced poems of courtly love (although the weather of Wales conspired against him often to comic effect), and of course his famous medieval Welsh erotic poems, of which this cywydd, 'Cywydd y Gal,' is a favorite of mine and of many others.

"Starting from a number of translations but relying strongly on Dafydd Johnston's, I've moved the poem back toward the cywydd form that Gwilym developed in fourteenth-century Wales. The more I work with the various translations of the poem and try to read it aloud in the original Welsh, the more I appreciate Gwilym's passion for sound, images, the world, and women. One thing that particularly delights me about this poem is how Gwilym manages to use the form to praise his penis and rebuke it at the same time. What man hasn't felt that way?"

Richard Jones was born in London, England, in 1953. His most recent book is *Apropos of Nothing* (Copper Canyon Press, 2006).

"The erotic is beyond language, and yet, like any reader, I apprehend its treasure through the electric truth of the senses. Language touches me, arouses me—my mind is awakened, my heart quickened. The Song of Solomon bears glad witness to a husband and wife who, in the world's lush garden, are God's most divine and vital creations. Sexual pleasure is God's gift to the marriage bed.

"But I am also drawn to stories like *Death in Venice,* or *Nadja,* or even 'The Artist of the Beautiful,' in which the erotic is idealized, and 'love' is a longing for Truth or Unveiled Mystery. Then I am a compassionate observer because, like the narrators of these tales, my soul is tantalized and wounded by the great quest. And yet how erotic it is when love—or is it imagination?—is tragically thwarted by madness or mortality, when human longing leads to disappointment, sorrow, and death.

"On the other hand, the binding to my copy of the life-charged *Tropic of Capricorn* is long broken, and the pages dog-eared and dirty."

Jane Kenyon (1947–1995). Born in Ann Arbor, Michigan, Kenyon was educated at the University of Michigan, where she met the poet Donald Hall. The couple married and moved to his family farm in rural New Hampshire in 1975. Their love story has become the stuff of local legend. After Hall was diagnosed with liver cancer, Kenyon wrote poems anticipating his demise. In "Pharaoh," for example, she wakes in the night with his "diminished bulk" beside her "like a sarcophagus." But Kenyon contracted leukemia in 1994 and died a little over a year later, and it was he who was left to write the poems of grief and loss. "The Shirt" makes an appearance in Hall's book *Without*: "Kate MacKay had me to supper / in Grafton, to read your poems / to our Hitchcock nurses. / Mary hooted when I read 'The Shirt.' / Walking to the car, I was happy / under the summer night, harsh / with stars."

Francis Scott Key (1780–1843). The man who wrote the words of America's national anthem was the district attorney for the District of Columbia when war broke out between the United States and Britain in 1812. On September 14, 1814, he witnessed the British bombardment of Baltimore from aboard the British prison frigate *Surprise*. He began writing the poem that became "The Star-Spangled Banner" when, despite hours of continual shelling, he saw the Stars and Stripes still flying above Fort McHenry at dawn. The Maryland native joined the Delphian Club of Baltimore in 1816 and regularly exchanged poems, puns, and toasts with fellow members. *Poems,* a posthumous collection, appeared in 1857. "On a Young Lady's Going into a Shower Bath" opens with a quotation from Hamlet's first major soliloquy.

Galway Kinnell was born in Providence, Rhode Island, in 1927.

"I would name D. H. Lawrence's 'Tortoise Shout.' It isn't exactly an erotic poem—except, of course, from the perspective of the tortoises."

Jennifer L. Knox was born in Lancaster, California, in 1968. In 2007 Bloof Books published her latest book of poems, *Drunk by Noon,* as well as a new edition of *A Gringo Like Me.*

Knox names *Oscar and Lucinda* by Peter Carey: "Intimate knowledge of another person is far more erotic to me than descriptions of sex—which can be about as sexy as a highly detailed lawn-mower manual."

Kenneth Koch (1925–2002). Koch (the name pronounced like the soft drink) was not only the funniest poet of his generation but possibly the one who did the most to dispel the notion that the ways and means of comedy and serious poetry are mutually exclusive. A Columbia professor whose books on pedagogy (such as *Rose, Where Did You Get That Red?*) revolutionized the teaching of poetry to schoolchildren, Koch adopted a jovially didactic persona in his 1975 collection *The Art of Love.* The lengthy title poem, a madcap spoof of Ovid, counsels the reader, who is assumed to be male, to "kiss as many women as you can" and experiment with bondage as foreplay. The poem remains Koch's most controversial: politically incorrect, offensive to some, but so hyperbolic and high-spirited it is hard to read as anything but a work of the comic imagination. Koch's advice to the man in love with a woman half his age is to add his and her age together, divide by two, and act as if both were the age represented by that number. This, he says, is called "Age Averaging."

Yusef Komunyakaa was born in Bogalusa, Louisiana, in 1947. His most recent book (with Chad Gracia) is *Gilgamesh: A Verse Play* (Wesleyan, 2006).

"For me, the erotic has to embrace innuendo and insinuation, and it begs the human imagination to participate. Everything isn't spelled out; the erotic is facilitated through suggestion. The sun shining through a thin, pale dress can be more provocative than an airbrushed frontal nude. Magic often resides in the hint, in that which is withheld. If beauty is the cornerstone of erotica, perhaps that explains why *The Arabian Nights* continue to beckon to me across the years."

Deborah Landau was born in Denver, Colorado, in 1967. Her most recent book is *Orchidelirium* (Anhinga Press, 2004).

"Frank O'Hara's 'Poem' ('À la recherche de Gertrude Stein') has the most gorgeous opening ('When I am feeling depressed and anxious sullen / all you have to do is take your clothes off / and all is wiped away revealing life's tenderness') and closing ('since once we are / together we always will be in this life come what may') lines. I read it to my husband at our wedding."

Dorianne Laux was born in Augusta, Maine, in 1952. Her most recent book is *Facts About the Moon* (W. W. Norton, 2005).

"I have loved and been influenced by the poems of D. H. Lawrence ('Whales Weep Not'), Carolyn Forché ('Reunion' and 'Kalaloch'), Sharon Olds, Ono no Komachi, and Li-Young Lee. But the piece I found most influential in writing 'The Shipfitter's Wife' was in a book called *The Gray Islands* by John Steffler (M&N Press, 1985), a Newfoundland writer who uses a broad range of forms and styles—lyrics, anecdotes, field notes, documents and pseudo-documents, ghost stories, tall tales—to tell the story of a man's isolation in a formidable landscape. Toward the end of the book, a couple he has only heard about share a bath for the first time. The simplicity of the language in Steffler's poem 'Carm' moved me to write a poem from the woman's perspective."

Emma Lazarus (1849–1887). Most famous for "The New Colossus," her sonnet that articulated the meaning and mission of the Statue of Liberty, Lazarus was the daughter of a prosperous Sephardic merchant in New York City. She corresponded with Emerson, translated Heine, and became, in response to news of vicious pogroms in Eastern Europe, a Zionist and champion of Jewish refugees. While she made a significant contribution to the history of the prose poem with such works as "The Exodus," she did her best work in the sonnet form. Unpublished until long after her death, "Assurance" is the most erotically explicit of her sonnets. "She wrote the poem as a dream vision and left it undated not to elude us but to redirect us," Esther Schor writes in *Emma Lazarus* (2006). "What the poem exposes is her unconscious, and it tells us that she met it—if not a female lover—face-to-face."

Amy Lowell (1874–1925). Born into a wealthy patrician family, Amy Lowell identified herself with the Imagist movement in poetry championed by Ezra Pound and H.D. (Hilda Doolittle). After Pound and Lowell fell out, he dismissed her version of their doctrine ("Amygism") and ridiculed her as a "hippopoetess," a reference to her chronic weight problem caused by a glandular condition. But Lowell was a far better poet than standard anthology representations imply. In 1912 she met the actress Ada Dwyer Russell, a widow eleven years her senior, who became her companion and lover. The relationship gave her the emotional support she needed to write her best poems, which display, in Honor Moore's phrase, "the bald audacity of her eroticism."

Sarah Maclay was born in Missoula, Montana, in 1956. Her most recent book is *The White Bride* (University of Tampa Press, 2008).

"I keep returning to W. S. Merwin's translation of Pablo Neruda's *Twenty Love Poems and a Song of Despair*—in part for sentimental reasons. Picking up this small blue volume—discovered, by chance, on a night table after wandering through the Valley of Fire—was a turning point that led me back to my own voice. Many years later, I was asked to read poem 'XIV' at my friend Dina's wedding, in a cathedral, and the words flew out of my mouth like wind, like birds, into the vastness. It was an astonishing experience. None of us could speak for more than a minute. To utter the words of the poem, to obey also its silences, is to enter a kind of magic. There is a lyric purity in these poems that seems to withstand even our age of irony. The degree to which Neruda trusts space and breath in his phrasing, his orchestration—and trusts, as well, the power of image, the power of metaphor, the power of synesthesia, the power of transformation of one thing to another—allows every border, between man and woman, between eras, between countries, between languages, between inner and external, to erode."

Sarah Manguso was born in Newton, Masschausetts, in 1974.

"I like Edward Gorey's *The Curious Sofa: A Pornographic Work* (1961), which he published under the pseudonym Ogdred Weary. The book's pornography is implied, and its readers are led to imagine every possible erotic pleasure and horror. 'Still later, Gerald did something terrible to Elsie with a saucepan.' Gorey illustrated the book just as suggestively."

Ross Martin was born in New Jersey in 1973. He is the author of *The Cop Who Rides Alone* (Zoo Press, 2002).

"Everything by Olga Broumas. She makes me feel like a natural woman."

Cate Marvin was born in Washington, D.C., in 1969. Her most recent book is *Fragment of the Head of a Queen* (Sarabande, 2007).

"Poem #520 by Emily Dickinson. The lover, as sea, spills its 'Pearl' into the speaker's shoes; she then meets him in the 'Solid Town.' I prefer sex in poems to be implied yet explicit, as opposed to graphic. Someone once successfully seduced me with this poem. I will always be grateful to him for turning me on to it. Unforgivable pun."

Bernadette Mayer (1945) was born in Brooklyn, New York, in 1945. Her most recent book is *Scarlet Tanager* (New Directions, 2005).

"I love and have always loved and been inspired by W. H. Auden's 'The Platonic Blow,' because it is great."

Editor's note: Auden's poem is included in *The Best American Erotic Poems* (see page 48).

Jeffrey McDaniel was born in Philadelphia in 1967. His most recent book of poems is *Splinter Factory* (Manic D Press, 2002).

"I don't know about favorites, but 'may i feel said he' by E. E. Cummings has a certain charge to it and could be exquisite read aloud in two voices."

Thomas McGrath (1916–1990). Born in Sheldon, North Dakota, McGrath studied in England as a Rhodes Scholar at Oxford University. He became a committed leftist during the Great Depression, was investigated by the FBI, and was later blacklisted after a defiantly uncooperative appearance before the House Un-American Activities Committee. Copper Canyon Press reissued his *Letter to an Imaginary Friend* in 1998.

Heather McHugh was born in San Diego, California, in 1948. Her books include *Eyeshot* (Wesleyan University Press, 2003).

"Archilochus was a soldier and a lover. Dating from the era soon after Homer, he wrote what would have been among the founding works known by literate Greeks. Thanks to the depredations of time and the deteriorations of papyrus, what we contemporary readers have of him are mere fragments—but what fragments! Full of spunk and blood, they suggest how powerful the conjunction of those two arenas (the battlefield and the bedroom) has been in human history. This latest fragment to be discovered (it was first published only in 1974) combines both of his characteristic fields—with aggressive elements (his denunciation of another woman) abutting tender ones (in the course of a young girl's deflowering). The result is what Guy Davenport called 'fireworks on the grass.' The friction in art between the intimate and the outright, the personal and the public, the lyric and the satiric, has always made sparks. The uncontainable sensual trembling of the girl (and the ejaculation of the man) reach us across the millennia (that the dead can tremble and come!). And a more cerebral factor—our knowledge that the text has survived into our day by virtue of its having been wrapped around a mummy—makes for the sort of contextual frisson only time can confer on an act of writing—as the Big Death wrapped its cloak around the Little One."

Here, in Davenport's translation (1995), are the last three stanzas of the fragment:

> I slid my arm under her neck
> To still the fear in her eyes,
> For she was trembling like a fawn,
>
> Touched her hot breasts with light fingers,
> Straddled her neatly and pressed
> Against her fine, hard, bared crotch.
>
> I caressed the beauty of all her body
> And came in a sudden white spurt
> While I was stroking her hair.

James Merrill (1926–1995). A son of the founder of the Merrill Lynch brokerage firm, James Merrill went to Amherst College, traveled a good deal, lived on several continents, befriended many younger writers, wrote novels and plays, and crafted a body of work that made him one of the major poets of his generation. A master of intricate forms and ingenious wordplay, he could elevate a spoonerism into an instrument of metaphysical wit: "The lean tree burst into grief." Merrill generated the material for *The Changing Light at Sandover,* his visionary epic of apocalypse and afterlife, from a thousand and one nights at the Ouija board with his partner David Jackson. Asked about this use of the Ouija board, Merrill said, "Don't you think there comes a time when everyone, not just a poet, wants to get beyond the self? To reach, if you like, the 'god' within you? The board, in however clumsy or absurd a way, allows for precisely that."

Noah Michelson was born in Racine, Wisconsin, in 1978.

"I remember reading Adrienne Rich's *21 Love Poems* when I was fifteen years old and finding, suspended in the thick of the other twenty poems dealing with love and loss and discovery and disappointment, '(The Floating Poem, Unnumbered).' I was mesmerized by Rich's ability to straddle two worlds—the sexual and the emotional—combining the graphic with the metaphorical, creating something beautiful and raw in the same space. Up until that point it had always seemed to be either/or, all or nothing, and I realized it didn't have to be that way, and usually, it wasn't—that the telling of the erotic, the telling of a certain kind of truth, could happen gracefully, honestly, and without fear."

Editor's note: Rich's poem is included in *The Best American Erotic Poems* (see page 103).

Edna St. Vincent Millay (1892–1950). "I am a harlot and a nun," Millay wrote when the sexual freedom she displayed in her life and her poems had become the stuff of gossip and rumor. Born in Rockland, Maine, on George Washington's birthday in 1892, Millay graduated from Vassar in 1917 and moved to Greenwich Village, where she gravitated to the center of a vivacious group of artists, writers, and actors. "She formulated for a new generation of young women a standard of sexual defiance and 'heroism' which, in spite of its romantic coloring, was marked by truth and pathos," Louise Bogan wrote, adding that Millay had the ability to transcend the faults to which she was prone, such as sentimentality and self-regard. "Many of her sonnets are in the great tradition; and that she was, by nature, a lyric poet of the first order, is an incontestable fact." In 1937 John Crowe Ransom criticized Millay's poetry for what he called "a deficiency in masculinity." It is a perplexing charge. The sonnet offered here is no less feminine for its use of a phallic image associated with such poets as William Butler Yeats and Hart Crane: the tower as a projection of the self.

Honor Moore was born in New York City in 1945. Her most recent book of poems is *Red Shoes* (W. W. Norton, 2005).

"I consider *The Story of O* by Pauline Réage to be one of the great works of the twentieth century. I like it for its purity, the directness of its female voice, its relentless insistence on the danger inherent in erotic hunger, the candor of its supplicating vulnerability—and for its revelation of what Brenda Shaughnessy has called 'the divine grief at the center of desire.' It was in response to Réage that I wrote 'Disparu,' which I consider a poem of erotic ebullience and sexual happiness."

Paul Muldoon was born in County Armagh, Northern Ireland, in 1951. His most recent book of poems is *Horse Latitudes* (Farrar, Straus and Giroux, 2006).

"It's hard to beat John Donne's 'On His Mistress Going to Bed' for the forensics of fornication."

Harryette Mullen was born in Florence, Alabama. Her most recent book is *Recyclopedia* (Graywolf Press, 2006).

"Some of my favorites are by Japanese writers: *The Tale of Genji* by Murasaki Shikibu, *The Pillow Book* by Sei Shonagon, Yasunari Kawabata's *Snow Country* and *House of the Sleeping Beauties*. A combination of frankness and indirection appeals to me, which is why I also enjoy the earthiness and double entendres of blues songs such as 'My Handyman' and 'Banana in Your Fruit Basket.'"

Frank O'Hara (1926–1966). "I am the least difficult of men," O'Hara once wrote. "All I want is boundless love." A central figure of the New York School of poets, he worked as a curator of painting at the Museum of Modern Art and dashed off poems during his lunch break. He wrote a monograph on Jackson Pollock and was planning retrospectives on Pollock and Willem de Kooning when he died of injuries sustained in a freak car accident on the beach at Fire Island. At his funeral, the painter Larry Rivers said that some sixty New Yorkers, himself among them, considered O'Hara to be their best friend. Rivers painted a huge *O'Hara Nude with Boots* in 1954, the year the poet wrote "To the Harbormaster" for Rivers.

Sharon Olds was born in San Francisco, California, in 1942. Her most recent book is *Strike Sparks: Selected Poems, 1980–2002* (Knopf, 2004).

"I guess one of my favorites would still be the Song of Songs—for so long, it was the only erotic writing I'd heard or seen. And there was something about that repetition—'I want to kiss you with the kisses of my mouth' (but now I look it up and see it is 'Let him kiss me with the kisses of his mouth'!)—as if there had been any other kisses the speaker could have kissed with! Even as a child, even in church—or especially as a child in church—I felt the power of that."

Danielle Pafunda was born in Albany, New York, in 1977. Her most recent book is *My Zorba* (Bloof Books, 2008).

"For educational value and kicks, my girlhood favorite hands down: *The Pearl (A Journal of Voluptuous Reading—the Underground Magazine of Victorian England)*. Epistles, odes, ditties, novellas, masquerades, nascent sexisms, pseudo-taboo, burgeoning hang-ups, absurd biologies, and all manner of sexing/sexualizing the soon-to-be modern lovers—including what must be the serialized debut of that wiggety-wack wishful thinking, *Fanny Hill*. Camp hyperbole, for sure, but every lewd, scintillating, scandalous, and fevered impulse of the twentieth century nestles inchoate in *The Pearl*. I literally split my crumbling 1979 edition (sadly out of print) with a friend on the eve of our college departures. Sarah, if this crosses your desk, I think it's time to trade halves."

Molly Peacock was born in Buffalo, New York, in 1947. Her books include *Cornucopia: New and Selected Poems 1975–2002* (2002).

"The inspiration for 'She Lays' is an erotic poem by the twelfth-century Chinese poet Li Ch'ing Chao, called 'To the Tune "Cutting a Flowering Plum Branch"' in the Kenneth Rexroth translation. It can be found in Rexroth's *Love and the Turning Year: One Hundred More Poems from the Chinese*. It's a pretty tame example of eros, but it's the first poem by a woman about a woman masturbating that I ever read, and it's still my favorite work of erotic writing. Here are the three lines that captured me in my early twenties, and still do: 'Gently I open / My silk dress and float alone / On the orchid boat.' I only sensed its subject at first, because it took me a while to discover that the orchid boat is a euphemism for female genitals, an image of a vulva. Some people find it difficult to look an actual orchid in the face for that reason. Li Ch'ing Chao's images, so solitary and so sensuous give a picture of what it is like to be alone with oneself in an erotic way, especially because the woman in the poem is ritualized and formal as she stages her art of masturbation. Inspired by her, I wrote 'She Lays' and even used the image of the orchid boat. When I wrote the poem, in my early thirties, I was reading a great deal of fiction, and I always wondered how the characters would masturbate. Disappointingly, none of the novelists ever said. But centuries before, Li Ch'ing Chao did and, because of Kenneth Rexroth, I was lucky enough to hear her."

Carl Phillips was born in Everett, Washington, in 1959. His most recent book is *Quiver of Arrows: Selected Poems 1986–2006* (Farrar, Straus and Giroux, 2007).

Phillips names Thom Gunn's "The Hug" and cites "how it looks at the intersection of trust, flesh, and the particular history that two people make between them—what continues to resonate, even past a later estrangement, between the two. To my mind, this is what pushes the erotic past sex, past geometry and physics."

Marge Piercy was born in Detroit, Michigan, in 1936. Her recent books are the novel *Sex Wars* (HarperPerennial), the poetry collection *The Crooked Inheritance* (Knopf), and *Pesach for the Rest of Us: Making the Passover Seder Your Own* (Schocken).

"'Salt in the Afternoon' is a summer poem. I have written many poems about love, about sex, about both. The imagery comes from the sea, of course, which we contain within us and which I live near—about a mile from the Bay and about a mile and a half from the ocean. All the shells are ones I have picked up walking on the beach. Locally, we are famous for oysters, and we have many squids and clams. The association between salt water and sex seems obvious to me. Our bodily fluids are salty.

"When I was very young, anything about sex could get me excited, including veiled references in the *Encyclopaedia Britannica*. When I was older, I liked well-written erotica. Now what I find most interesting are the women's fantasies collected by Nancy Friday over the years and published in various collections. What other women fantasize about interests me far more than most polished erotic writings. I also find erotic fan writings sometimes fascinating. None of these is really designed for an audience, so there is something potent and uncensored about them. We all know about men's sexual fantasies, but women's are a much more obscure subject."

Sylvia Plath was born in Boston. She graduated summa cum laude from Smith College and won a Fulbright to Cambridge University, where she met and married the English poet (and future poet laureate) Ted Hughes. Plath's actual father taught German at Boston University, wrote a treatise on bees, and died when his daughter was only eight. Nevertheless, the poet wrote a ferocious assault on "Daddy," whom she depicts, in the poem of that title, as a fascist and a brute. In her journals, published in 2000, Plath wrote about the first time she and Hughes had sex ("Washed my battered face, smeared with a purple bruise from Ted"), making a mental note to "consider yourself lucky to have been stabbed by him." Plath separated from Hughes in October 1962 and took her own life four months later.

Edgar Allan Poe (1809–1849). As a young man, Poe, the inventor of the detective story and peerless teller of tales of terror, had courted and wanted to marry his childhood sweetheart, Sarah Elmira Royster. The engagement was broken off after Poe entered the University of Virginia, where he lasted one year, accumulating gambling debts that his foster father refused to pay. Sarah Royster married another man, and Poe wrote "Tamerlane," "Bridal Ballad," "Sonnet to Zante," and possibly "Annabel Lee" about this early love and loss. The poem beginning "I saw thee on thy bridal day" was written at the time of Sarah's wedding in 1827, with final revisions made in 1845. Poe's love survived marriages and decades. In the last year of his life, he became engaged to Sarah, then a widow, for the second time.

H. Phelps Putnam (1894–1948). According to his friend Edmund Wilson, Howard Phelps Putnam "was—rather like E. E. Cummings—fatally attractive to women." At Yale, Putnam won election to the Skull and Bones secret society on the basis of "his not voluminous poetry, his personal charm and his obvious superiority," and in New York in the 1920s he could philander with the best of them. "I remember once visiting his rooms in New York when I was going to have dinner with him," Wilson wrote. "As he was putting on his shirt, he displayed, with conscious pride, his bare back, which was streaked with what, rather shocked, I took for the results of some masochistic whipping, not knowing then that women, in their passion, sometimes thus ripped their lovers' backs. But he wrote of his women in such a way as must sometimes have made them uneasy." Around 1927 Putnam met the actress Katharine Hepburn, then a student at Bryn Mawr College. His relationship with her differed from his usual brand of female conquest and may have inspired him to write "The Daughters of the Sun": "She was the living anarchy of love, / She was the unexplained, the end of love, / The one who occupies the dreamy self, / The one appearance in the finite world / Which is seen by us one time, and then despaired / Beyond romantic comfort afterwards." Putnam's health declined, and he wrote little after the second of his two collections (*The Five Seasons*) appeared in 1931.

Michael Quattrone was born in Concord, Massachusetts, in 1977.

"*The Fermata* by Nicholson Baker. I can never decide which is more exciting, the scenes Baker depicts or the language he uses to achieve them. The greatness of *The Fermata* is that its arousals are synchronous. The acuity of the author's observation finds outlet in the compulsive voyeurism of his protagonist-narrator, just as Arno Strine's adventures in a paused universe suggest the reader's solitary delinquency as he or she indulges in another chapter. The metafictional unfolding of the novel, and the rapturous coinages and appropriations it contains, prove that the imagination is a fetishist."

Kenneth Rexroth (1905–1982). When Rexroth published *The Love Poems of Marichiko,* he announced that they were the work of a "contemporary young woman who lives near the temple of Marishi-be in Kyoto" and that he was merely the work's translator. But though he had translated entire volumes of Chinese and Japanese poetry written exclusively by women, Marichiko was his invention, and Rexroth, when pressed, did not deny his authorship of these "love poems." There are several ironies at work here. In his own poems, Rexroth had celebrated, from the male perspective, the female body and "the sweet secret odor of sex," yet as an old man he expressed his deepest erotic feelings through the persona of a young Japanese woman. The Marichiko poems demonstrate the attractions of the pseudo-translation (or hoax translation) as a method of verse composition as well as, perhaps, a means of self-discovery.

Adrienne Rich was born in Baltimore, Maryland, in 1929. Her most recent book is *Telephone Ringing in the Labyrinth: Poems 2004–2006* (W. W. Norton, 2007).

"I don't believe in favorites. All poetry worthy of the name is erotic."

Muriel Rukeyser (1913–1980). Born in New York City, Rukeyser was passionately political, an advocate of left-wing causes from the Spanish civil war in the 1930s to feminism in the 1960s. "If there were no poetry on any day in the world, poetry would be invented that day," she wrote. "For there would be an intolerable hunger." Anne Sexton and Adrienne Rich were among the poets inspired by Rukeyser's example. "No more masks!" she declared. The line became a feminist rallying cry and the title of an anthology devoted to twentieth-century American women poets.

James Schuyler (1923–1991). Born in Chicago, Schuyler lived in New York City, where he associated with the artists and writers of the New York School. In the early 1950s, Kenneth Koch commented, "Jimmy was a regular part of our gang," along with the poets John Ashbery and Frank O'Hara and the painters Jane Freilicher and Larry Rivers. "If you invited one of us to a party, you were likely to get us all, plus one or two more," Koch wrote. "We were each other's main audience and so in time each other's main inspiration." Ashbery (in collaboration with whom Schuyler wrote the comic novel *A Nest of Ninnies*) introduced the first public poetry reading the shy and nervous Schuyler ever gave. It took place in November 1988. "It's nice to have a writer to whom one feels so close both personally and aesthetically that asking advice from him is only a step removed from consulting oneself," Ashbery said that night. But he was "jealous" of Schuyler's singularity, he added. "He makes sense, dammit, and he manages to do so without falsifying or simplifying the daunting complexity of life as we are living it today."

Frederick Seidel was born in St. Louis, Missouri, in 1936. His most recent book is *Ooga-Booga* (Farrar, Straus and Giroux, 2006).

Peter Serchuk was born in Queens, New York, in 1952. His most recent book is *Waiting for Poppa at the Smithtown Diner* (University of Illinois Press, 1990).

"My apologies to Anaïs Nin and Henry Miller, both of whom I've enjoyed immensely. However, I think my favorite is *My Secret Life* by Anonymous. I first read it as a teenager and was overwhelmed not only by its graphic sexual adventures (all under the radar in Victorian England) but perhaps even more so by its precise and graphic language. Hearing masturbation described as 'frigging myself' and withdrawal after intercourse as 'uncunted' was almost as titillating to my aspiring writer's ear as it was to my thermal imagination."

Anne Sexton (1928–1974). Anne Sexton and Sylvia Plath have more than a little in common. Both came under the direct influence of Robert Lowell, embraced the "confessional" style, disclosed intimate personal details, and took their own lives. Because comparisons are inevitable, Sexton has sometimes seemed like a lesser version of the iconic Plath, who predeceased her by a decade. In fact, Sexton has major strengths all her own, including an unabashed sexuality; the singular passion in such poems as "The Fury of Cocks" and "When Man Enters Woman" is in keeping with the first syllable of the poet's last name. The poem in two stanzas given here begins with a barrier separating the lovers and ends in their union on "the identical river called Mine."

Ravi Shankar was born in Washington, D.C., in 1975. His most recent book is *Instrumentality* (Cherry Grove, 2004).

"In the twelfth century, Jayadeva of Orissa wrote the Sanskrit lyric poem the *Gita Govinda*, which rhapsodized the romance of Krishna, butter thief and divine cowherd, and his beloved, Radha. Back from cavorting with the gopis, Krishna is met with the sensual fury of Radha, who is described as having heaving breasts, kohl-darkened eyes, jangling anklets, and a lotus mouth (what I wouldn't do for a lotus mouth!). Begging for her forgiveness, Krishna entreats Radha to chain him and bite him, to pulverize him in her curves. That's got to be my favorite work of erotic writing; it is simultaneously transgressive and ardent, secretive and arousing, fraught with the full import of sexuality as a creative, carnal, pulsing act, something as deeply spiritual as it is resolutely corporeal. Radha's erotic, even illicit, feelings for Krishna are the very equivalent of religious passion."

Brenda Shaughnessy was born in Okinawa, Japan, in 1970. Her most recent book is *Human Dark with Sugar* (Copper Canyon Press, 2008).

"My favorite is Gertrude Stein's *Lifting Belly*. This book-length poem is not only beautiful and incantatory, and more than a little shocking, but it is also utter nonsense, which strikes me as sort of super-erotic. When I'm lucky enough to happen upon language that is totally illogical, cagey, and secretive, and yet sensorily suffused and extraordinarily insistent, another part of my mind springs to life, a part that is neither all mental nor all physical, and yet not suspended in the strange limbo of the 'spiritual,' but fully immersed in the erotic, that is, the realm of imagination, floating images, private meanings and associations."

Editor's note: See page 26 for an excerpt from Stein's *Lifting Belly*.

Rachel Shukert was born in Omaha, Nebraska, in 1980. Her latest book, a collection of essays, is *Have You No Shame?* (Villard, 2008).

"*Chocolates for Breakfast* by Pamela Moore is not an erotic work per se; it's a product of an all-too-brief vogue for novels about sexually precocious poor little rich girls, written by sexually precocious poor little rich girls (see Sagan, Françoise). It is, in fact, sort of an American *Bonjour Tristesse,* this time set against the cocktail-party swirl of 1950s Manhattan and Hollywood, complete with alcoholic writers, suicidal debutantes, and fresh-faced Yale boys with One Thing On Their Minds. The sexual conquests of the fifteen-year-old protagonist include a closeted B-movie actor drowning in a sea of gin and torment; the louche, Byronic scion of minor European aristocracy; and a witty, cold-blooded WASP looking down his nose at the whole sad affair—coincidentally, precisely the types of men who have figured into every one of my meaningful sexual fantasies. As a result, the demurely written love scenes, even filled with torpid references to the sea and the sun, are some of the hottest things I have ever read. Honorable mention goes to *The Happy Hooker* by Xaviera Hollander, for teaching me everything I know, and of course, Butler's *Lives of the Saints,* which requires no explanation."

Richard Siken was born in New York City in 1967. His book *Crush* won the Yale Younger Poets Prize and appeared from Yale University Press in 2005.

"For me, the erotic is uncomfortable: a friction produced when the life of the mind rubs up against the life of the body. I'd rather live the life of the mind. Exclusively. It can't be done. The life of the body is base and gross. It's pornography, really: mucky organics convulsing plotlessly in overlit rooms. The body is a tragedy. It is not the life of the mind that craves Super Nachos and wears hot pants. Dennis Cooper understands this. His poem 'My Past' is dirty and mean-spirited. It also attempts to reconcile mind and body. I could quote every line and yammer on about tonal texture, direct address, and sadness disguised as huff and bluster, but here's my favorite part: 'Take you, for example, who I found throwing up in the bathroom of some actor's mansion and crowned my new boyfriend.' The conflation of the body's betrayal of itself (vomiting in the throne of the toilet) with the mind's grandiose romantic coronation of the boyfriend is, for me, perfect. We want, and we hate that we want, and we embarrass ourselves with it and about it, and we want it all to be pretty but only part of it is pretty, a small part, if that, and we want it more than anything but thinking about it just makes our heads hurt. Thank you, Dennis Cooper. I could kiss you."

Charles Simic was born in Belgrade, Yugoslavia, in 1938. In August 2007 he was appointed Poet Laureate of the United States. His recent books include *My Noiseless Entourage* (Harcourt, 2005) and *The Voice at 3:00 A.M.: Selected Late and New Poems* (Harcourt, 2003).

"Ovid's *Amores* are my ideal of love poetry. Lyrical, witty, psychologically acute, and erotic, the poems, in Peter Green's gorgeous translation, are a work of great literature. Ovid knew that what happens between the sheets is most often the stuff of low comedy. As for tragedy, he pleaded:

> Just be patient awhile. Your service
> Demands a lifetime. Her needs are quickly met."

Louis Simpson was born in Jamaica, West Indies, in 1923. His most recent book is *The Owner of the House: New Collected Poems, 1940–2001* (BOA Editions, 2003).

"It has to be James Joyce's *Ulysses*. Sorry to disappoint the heavy breathers. I would also name Flaubert's *Madame Bovary.*"

Ed Smith (1957–2005). Edward Young Smith was born in Queens, New York. As a teen, he had aspired to become a theoretical physicist specializing in graviton propagation, and he attended Pomona College for two years. In the 1980s he joined the group of writers and artists—such as Dennis Cooper, David Trinidad, Bob Flanagan, Amy Gerstler, and Benjamin Weissman—who congregated at the Beyond Baroque literary arts center in Venice, California. He and his wife, the artist Mio Shirai, moved to New York in 1997, where he worked as a computer animator for the children's television program *Blue's Clues* on MTV.

Gertrude Stein (1874–1946). No other American writer born in the nineteenth century was as unrelentingly innovative as Gertrude Stein; she has outdone her most ardent disciples in radical experimentation. Stein, who studied with William James at Radcliffe, settled in Paris in 1903 and met Alice B. Toklas four years later. Their studio at 27 rue de Fleurus became an international artistic salon, a mandatory destination for ambitious American writers. Lecturing at the University of Chicago, Stein was asked about her line "rose is a rose is a rose." "I notice that you all know it," Stein said. "You make fun of it, but you know it. Now listen! I know that in daily life we don't go around saying '. . . is a . . . is a . . . is a . . . .' Yes, I'm no fool; but I think that in that line the rose is red for the first time in English poetry for a hundred years."

Wallace Stevens (1879–1955). Born in Reading, Pennsylvania, Stevens studied at Harvard, became a lawyer, and married a girl from his hometown, Elsie Kachel Moll, who modeled for the figures on the Mercury dime and the Liberty half-dollar. For most of his life the poet worked as an executive for the Hartford Accident and Indemnity Company, becoming a vice president in 1934. Never learning how to drive, Stevens walked the two miles between his Hartford home and office twice daily, composing poems in his head. "Peter Quince at the Clavier" retells the biblical story of Susanna and the Elders, from the apocryphal book of Daniel. In the tale, the married heroine rebuffs the leering advances of two aging voyeurs. In revenge, the men accuse her of lewdness. They are stoned to death when it is determined that they are lying. The musical motifs throughout the poem suggest that music (or music as a metonymy of art) is the poem's true subject, yet it remains Stevens's most erotic work, culminating in a meditation on beauty and the human body. An inveterate aphorist, Stevens once observed that "A poet looks at the world the way a man looks at a woman."

Ruth Stone was born in Roanoke, Virginia, in 1915. Her most recent book is *In the Dark* (Copper Canyon Press, 2004). A new and selected poems entitled *What Loves Comes To* is forthcoming from Copper Canyon in 2008.

"My favorite erotic poem is 'Compelled to Love' by my husband, Walter Stone, published after his death in 1959, in Scribner's Poets of Today series, volume VI. Sensual, romantic, and beautifully constructed, it captures both the rapture and the universality of the act of love. To demonstrate, the following is a condensed quote from the poem:

"'Compelled to love, his body sings . . . He probes her jewel-box . . . With the same instrument that kings . . . Unlock their queens with . . . The classic key that fits their golden wives.'"

Mark Strand was born in Summerside, Prince Edward Island, Canada, in 1934. His most recent book is *New Selected Poems* (Knopf, 2007).

"I have not read anything recently that qualifies as erotic. When I was a teenager, I read the scatological poems and, I suppose, considered them mildly erotic—but much 'dirtier' than erotic. Some poems of Robert Burns, also in the dirty-joke category. But nothing else. I never thought *Lady Chatterley's Lover* particularly erotic; *The Story of O*, I suppose, was. But I read those books so long ago I am not sure what my reaction to them was."

May Swenson (1913–1989). Swenson grew up as the eldest of ten children in a Swedish-speaking Mormon household in Logan, Utah. She wrote sexy poems on subjects ranging from carnal knowledge to films based on Ian Fleming's spy novels ("The James Bond Movie") and the national pastime ("Analysis of Baseball"). She remains an undervalued treasure. Richard Wilbur wrote that Swenson "trusted her craving to go beyond the self and her rapture in making imaginative fusions with the other. In consequence, her poems find the erotic in all forms of natural energy and, whether they speak of nebulae or horses or human love, are full of a wonderfully straightforward and ebullient sexuality."

John Updike was born in West Reading, Pennsylvania, in 1932. His most recent book is *Due Considerations: Essays and Criticism* (Knopf, 2007).

Updike names "*Her* by (I think) Anonymous. It contains some real sexual psychology."

Paul Violi was born in New York City in 1944. His most recent book of poems is *Overnight* (Hanging Loose Press, 2007).

"A popular choice, I bet, though it has had its share of silly detractors over the last couple of decades, Andrew Marvell's 'To His Coy Mistress' is one of my favorite short poems, erotic or otherwise. It's so full of life, it reads like a short play, a dramatized syllogism, wildly passionate and irrefutably logical. Witty, allusive, intimate, sexy, playful, serious, intense—the tonal shifts, imagery, and sheer artistry are stunning. Ornithologists are not convinced that mating eagles clutch, tumble, and cannonball down the sky, but I still think Marvell got it right."

William Wadsworth was born in New York City in 1950. *The Physicist on a Cold Night Explains,* a chapbook, was published by Breakaway Press in 2002.

"My favorite piece of erotic writing is the collection of poems by Paul Verlaine entitled *Femmes/Hombres,* which was not published in full until the 1970s because the poems were considered too scandalous until then to see the light of day. The book (published in English in Alistair Elliot's translation under the title *Men/Women*) is, quite simply, the dirtiest book I know. Not only does Verlaine (on occasion in collaboration with Rimbaud) write equally enthusiastically about heterosexual and homosexual love (between both sexes), but he treats with particularly earthy relish some erotic practices still considered today to be on the margins of sexual taboo. My runner-up would be 'The True Confession of George Barker,' by one of the great neglected bad-boy poets of England. The book-length poem is a rollicking Byronic tour de force written in the stanzas of Villon's testament; it was banned in England when it was first published in 1950 and almost brought down the BBC for broadcasting a reading from it."

Catherine Wagner was born in Rangoon, Burma (now Myanmar). Her most recent book is *Macular Hole* (Fence, 2004).

"Anything by Robert Herrick, for the roughness of his verbs (which are dressed in silk, but barely). Also, *Ada, or Ardor* by Vladimir Nabokov, because the narrator makes his beloved and me both squirm, she with passion, I with titillated annoyance. Squirming should always happen in layers. And finally, for delaying my gratification to an absurd degree, 1960s romance novels about nurses, such as *Emergency Nurse,* by Peggy Gaddis, 1963 ('"You're a very nice girl!" Dr. Latimer said.')."

David Wagoner was born in Massillon, Ohio, in 1926. *A Map of the Night* will be published by the University of Illinois Press in early spring 2008.

"My favorite erotic poem is 'No Platonic Love' by William Cartwright (1611–1643). It's a very modern-seeming poem from three and a half centuries ago. Four stanzas of exactly rhymed, conversationally easy metrical poetry, witty and wise, and throughout, the poet maintains his own unmistakable voice. Such pieces, erotic or otherwise, are not very common in English or American poetry. It's as rhetorically balanced as the best of John Donne, a number of whose erotic poems are also favorites of mine."

Maggie Wells was born in Mission Viejo, California, in 1977. Her chapbook *Corey Feldman and the Flamingo, a Dialogue: The Struggles of an Icon* was published by PressBody Press in 2007.

" 'Hot Ass Poem' by Jennifer L. Knox first reads as a satire of the type of man who wanders the streets frothing at the mouth over every ass crossing his path. Sure, it is hilarious and ridiculous as written. To me, though, 'Hot Ass Poem' is super-erotic. This block of rambling, building (nearly to climax) text is so very animalistic in its obsession with the ass that the actual owner of the ass becomes irrelevant. Crazed with lust, the narrator moves from ass to ass to ass (a human, a dog, even a building) like a bloodhound tracking prey. One reason humans evolved into nearly bald creatures is that apes with more prominent asses (preferably bald, pink, and swollen) attract the most mates. This poem pulls from the essence of attraction in that sense, and dives deep into the wet core of primal eroticism."

Edith Wharton (1862–1937). The author of *The Age of Innocence* and *The House of Mirth* wrote "Terminus" in 1909 after a "secret night" of intense lovemaking with Morton Fullerton, the American-born correspondent for the London *Times*, whom the unhappily married novelist had met two years earlier and with whom she had fallen hopelessly in love. Fullerton was as suave as he was unreliable, a seducer adept at breaking hearts. The couple spent the night of June 4 in Suite 92 of the Charing Cross Hotel in London. The next morning Fullerton sailed for New York. In later years he maintained that Wharton began writing "Terminus" in bed that night in a postcoital rush. Commenting on the poem, Wharton's biographer Hermione Lee notes that Wharton "does not quite say that spending the night with her lover in a railway hotel makes her feel like a prostitute, but she does want to identify with the women before her who may also have lain awake all night listening to the orgasmic 'night-long shudder of traffic' and 'the farewell shriek of the trains.' Like them, she has to face the 'terminus': the ending of the night and the journey onwards under 'the hand of implacable fate.' " In her journal, Wharton, then forty-six, wrote, "I have drunk the wine of life at last. I have known the thing best worth knowing."

Walt Whitman (1819–1892). Whitman celebrates the body with unabashed ardor, believing it to be holy. "The scent of these arm-pits is aroma finer than prayer," he writes in "Song of Myself." In the first edition of *Leaves of Grass* (1855), "I Sing the Body Electric" lacked the phrase that became its title, which Whitman added a year later, along with the entire last section of the poem. Today the homoerotic dimension of his work is generally recognized. Noting that "Song of Myself" has many passages that are "clearly masturbatory and jismatic," Jeffrey Meyers calls Whitman "Wally the Wonker." Harold Bloom sounds less scornful: Whitman "proudly speaks for Onan. As a god, Walt resembles an Egyptian deity masturbating a cosmos into existence." As a man, he offers the virtues of a democratic vision ("it is as great to be a woman as to be a man") and the promised liberation of American poetry from the yoke of received tradition ("I sound my barbaric yawp over the roofs of the world"). In his prose foreword to the 1855 edition of *Leaves of Grass,* Whitman says that one true test of a poem is whether it might "help breed one goodshaped and well-hung man, and a woman to be his perfect and independent mate." His influence is boundless. It is apparent not only in the Allen Ginsberg poem in this volume but in Wallace Stevens's assertion that "the greatest poverty is not to live in a physical world" and A. R. Ammons's belief in an illuminating "radiance" that looks unflinchingly into "the guiltiest / swervings of the weaving heart."

Richard Wilbur was born in New York City in 1921. His most recent books are *Collected Poems 1943–2004* (Harcourt, 2004) and a translation of *Pierre Corneille: The Theatre of Illusion* (Harcourt, 2007).

"The erotic is most attractive when it is not impersonal, but accompanied by love or affection. It is important that Julia's name appears in the title of such a poem as 'Upon the Nipples of Julia's Breast,' by Robert Herrick."

C. K. Williams was born in Newark, New Jersey, in 1936. His *Collected Poems* appeared from Farrar, Straus and Giroux in 2006.

"Shakespeare's 'Venus and Adonis' is one of the sexiest pieces of writing ever, while at the same time it makes wise and gentle mockery of our helplessness before the force of lust. It's also very funny, and sad, and Shakespearean, which means poetically lavish and openly and elaborately and rapturously carnal. Here, for example, thwarted Venus to her Adonis:

'I'll be a park, and thou shalt be my deer;
Feed where thou wilt, on mountain or in dale;
   Graze on my lips; and if those hills be dry,
   Stray lower, where the pleasant fountains lie.'"

Lisa Williams was born in Nashville, Tennessee, in 1966. Her second volume of poems, *Woman Reading to the Sea,* is forthcoming from W. W. Norton in 2008.

"Regarding erotic writing, I've always liked that of Anaïs Nin. Her erotica is fearless, imaginative, and strange—like dangerous but very interesting dreams: You know you should wake up, but you don't quite want to. And she can be both raunchy and delicate; much erotic writing seems to indulge in one or the other to a limiting extreme. I like to think the two can coexist, and I hope I make that a little evident in my poem."

Tennessee Williams (1911–1983). The world knows Tennessee Williams (born in Columbus, Mississippi) as a major playwright, but he also considered himself a poet, publishing two volumes of poetry during his lifetime: *In the Winter of Cities* (1956) and *Androgyne, Mon Amour* (1977). Like his plays, Williams's poems shiver with pathos, move with dramatic tension, and express a sardonic wit. He idolized Hart Crane, lifting the title of his play *Summer and Smoke* from Crane's "Emblems of Conduct," and quoting from Crane's "The Broken Tower" for the epigraph of *A Streetcar Named Desire.* The living, burning, crying struggle that he admires in Crane's poetry is what Williams explores throughout his own oeuvre, from his portrait of Blanche DuBois to the two nameless lovers in the poem included here.

William Carlos Williams (1883–1963). Dr. Williams supported his family as a pediatrician in the town of his birth, Rutherford, New Jersey; he would write poems between house calls and hospital visits. "A poem is a small (or large) machine made of words," Williams wrote. "It isn't what [the poet] *says* that counts as a work of art, it's what he makes, with such intensity of perception that it lives with an intrinsic movement of its own to verify its authenticity." Williams committed himself to colloquial idioms and rhythms, and his best poems can serve as object lessons in the value of lining and line breaks in free verse. In his book *On Being Blue,* William Gass argues that sex enters writing in any of several ways, including "direct depiction," the use of "sexual words," "displacement" (the use of metaphor), and "the use of language like a lover." Like the rock in Conrad Aiken's "Sea Holly," the tree in "Young Sycamore" is an energetic instance of what Gass calls "displacement." By the end of the poem, the phallic tree seems to have become a satyr with a horn on top.

Catherine Wing was born in New York City in 1972. Her first book of poems, *Enter Invisible,* was published by Sarabande Books in 2005.

"My favorite piece of erotic writing—perhaps better described as writing that's glancingly erotic—is the sonnet 'Winter Wheat' by Paul Muldoon. To risk, as Frost would have it, saying the poem in worse English: The narrator is outside with a woman in the preliminary stages of a sexual encounter as he watches a plowboy off in a distant field. If playboy watching plowboy seems not enough to warrant arousal, the poem ever so delicately unbuttons its not so subtle rhymes (lobe/globe, groan/roan, urge/splurge) with the sexiest syntax, two parts delay, one part awkward advance—just as sex outside with a stranger might be. But my favorite, and no doubt the weirdest element of the poem, is all the borderline-prelingual *somethings* that clutter up and stagger about in twelve of the poem's fourteen lines: 'The plowboy was something his something' or 'in her something something ruff' or 'I might have something the something groan / of the something plowboy. . . .' There is no greater crippler of language than sexual desire, and even as I'm never exactly sure what those mysterious 'something somethings' are, I know I want more than some of it."

Cecilia Woloch was born in Pittsburgh, Pennsylvania, in 1956. Her most recent book is *Late* (BOA Editions, 2003).

"I may be confusing the erotic with the romantic, but I think the debt 'Bareback Pantoum' owes to the old Alfred Noyes poem 'The Highwayman' is pretty obvious. The dictionary defines *erotic* as 'arousing sexual desire or excitement,' and *romantic* as 'suggestive of the feeling of excitement and mystery associated with love,' so the two aren't really so far apart. I first encountered 'The Highwayman' as an impressionable adolescent, but it still makes me swoon—its darkness and danger and rhythm; the obsessive quality of the repetition; the mysteriousness and beauty of the imagery. And yet there's only that one kiss in all the poem: the landlord's black-eyed daughter loosening her cascade of hair over his breast and the highwayman kissing its waves in the moonlight. Maybe all romantic love is in some way doomed, and sexual love is, of course, so entwined with physical mortality; but it seems to me that longing—and here's a whole landscape of longing—makes us feel most deeply and achingly alive."

C. Dale Young was born in London, England, in 1969. His latest book of poems is *The Second Person* (Four Way Books, 2007).

"I remember quite well both the shock and glee I felt when I first read E. M. Forster's *Maurice*. I was seventeen at the time, and I had never read anything that had, at its core, same-sex love. I had no idea such novels existed, much less novels written by 'great' writers like Forster. For this reason, despite its somewhat tame storyline considering the contemporary lust for the graphic, *Maurice* remains my favorite. It opened my eyes to so many possibilities."

Dean Young was born in Columbia, Pennsylvania, in 1955. His most recent book is *embryoyo* (Believer Books, 2007).

"'Reciprocal love, the only kind that should concern us here,' begins the section 'Love' in André Breton and Paul Éluard's surrealist collaboration *The Immaculate Corpse*. What follows is a surrealist *Kama Sutra* in which various positions are given marvelous and funny names. 'When the woman is on her back and the man lies on top of her it is *cedilla*.' The distinction between erotica and pornography is legalese, useless and impossible, while sexual energy is always everpossible and variously useful to the debacle of use. A funny thing happens to language when it gets in the realm of sex: It defies whatever divorce we abstract of sign from signified and becomes oversaturated with referent, flushed so that nearly any word not only refers to its object, action, or state, but also some wondrous, lubricious arrangement of limbs, of mouths. Virginia creeper. Opening a window. In Éluard and Breton's uproarious, horny catalog, it is as if Adam (forgive the phallocentric moment, or rather, allow the phallocentric its turn), when he was about naming the things of the world, was really naming all the things he'd done, wanted to do, with Eve simultaneously. (For one of Eve's versions, I recommend Gertrude Stein's *Lifting Belly*.) What are the famously surreal umbrella and sewing machine doing on that operating table, anyway? Making love, of course, said Max Ernst."

Editor's note: See page 26 for an excerpt from Stein's *Lifting Belly.*

Kevin Young was born in Lincoln, Nebraska in 1970. His most recent book is *For the Confederate Dead* (Knopf, 2007).

"I'm not sure I have a favorite work of erotic writing—but my favorite bit of agape writing is probably Dante's *La Vita Nuova.* In its balance not just of emotion and analysis but of poetry and prose, 'The New Life' manages to capture a full range of feeling—to be 'new' in terms of both form and feeling. There's something awfully erotic about that."

ACKNOWLEDGMENTS

Heartfelt thanks go to my colleague Mark Bibbins and to the various assistants and advisers I enlisted for this project. I came to depend on Nick Adamski, Jill Baron, Laura Cronk, Steven Dube, Sarah Ruth Jacobs, and Michael Quattrone for suggestions, opinions, and research. An editor needs all the help he can get, and it gives me pleasure to acknowledge the many other individuals who made recommendations or gave me the benefit of their thinking. The list includes Nin Andrews, Molly Arden, Sally Ashton, Danielle Ben-Veniste, Erin Burke, Brian Carey Chung, Siobhan Ciminera, Victoria Clausi, Marc Cohen, Billy Collins, James Cummins, Peter Davis, Elaine Equi, Erica Miriam Fabri, Jenny Factor, Amy Gerstler, Roger Gilbert, Anna Ojascastro Guzon, Judith Hall, Stacey Harwood, Jennifer Michael Hecht, Tony Hoagland, John Hollander, Ron Horning, Richard Howard, Deborah Landau, Reb Livingston, Sarah Maclay, Cate Marvin, Alexandra Mendez-Diez, Honor Moore, Geoffrey O'Brien, Karl Parker, Megan Punschke, Allyson Salazar, Liesel Tarquini, Lee Upton, William Wadsworth, Matthew Yeager, Stephen Young, and Matthew Zapruder. In my graduate literature seminar at the New School in spring 2007, we devoted two sessions to a consideration of contenders for inclusion in this book. The students who engaged in this candid discussion merit acknowledgment: Komo Ananda, Jaclyn Clark, Julia Cohen, Jennifer Fortin, P. J. Gallo, Evan Glasson, Yotam Hasass, Kathleen Khouri, Christie Ann Reynolds, Paige Taggart, and Michael Wilson. For help in locating contributors, thanks go to Billy Merrell and Robin Beth Schaer of the Academy of American Poets. For an account of his experience publishing Auden's "The Platonic Blow," I am indebted to Roger Lathbury. Fred Courtright handled permissions with aplomb.

As ever I am indebted to my agents, Glen Hartley and Lynn Chu of Writers' Representatives, and to Molly Dorozenski, Erich Hobbing, and Daniel Cuddy of Scribner. Alexis Gargagliano worked closely on this project from the start, easing its progress from conception to delivery. I am very lucky to have her as my editor.

Grateful acknowledgment is made of the publications from which the poems in this volume were chosen. A sincere attempt has been made to locate all copyright holders. Unless specifically stated otherwise, copyright to the poems is held by the individual poets.

Kim Addonizio: "The Divorcée and Gin" from *Tell Me*. Copyright (c) 2000 by Kim Addonizio. Reprinted with the permission of BOA Editions, Ltd., www.boaeditions.org.

Ai: "Twenty-Year Marriage" from *Vice: New and Selected Poems*. Copyright (c) 1999 by Ai. Reprinted with the permission of W. W. Norton & Company, Inc.

Conrad Aiken: "Sea Holly" from *Selected Poems*, Oxford University Press. Copyright (c) 1961 by Conrad Aiken, renewed (c) 1989 by Mary Hoover Aiken. Reprinted by permission of Brandt & Hochman Literary Agents, Inc.

Sandra Alcosser: "By the Nape" from *Except by Nature*. Copyright (c) 1998 by Sandra Alcosser. Reprinted with the permission of Graywolf Press.

Elizabeth Alexander: "At Seventeen." Used with the permission of the author.

A. R. Ammons: "Their Sex Life" from *The Really Short Poems of A. R. Ammons*. Copyright (c) 1990 by A. R. Ammons. Reprinted with the permission of W. W. Norton & Company, Inc.

Nin Andrews: "How to Have an Orgasm: Examples" from *The Book of Orgasms*. Copyright (c) 2000 by Nin Andrews. Reprinted with the permission of the Cleveland State University Poetry Center.

Sarah Arvio: "Mirrors" from *Visits from the Seventh*. Copyright (c) 2002 by Sarah Arvio. Reprinted with the permission of Alfred A. Knopf, a division of Random House, Inc.

Ellen Bass: "Gate C22" from *The Human Line*. Copyright (c) 2007 by Ellen Bass. Reprinted with the permission of Copper Canyon Press, www.copper canyonpress.org.

Ted Berrigan: "Dinner at George & Katie Schneeman's" from *The Collected Poems of Ted Berrigan*. Copyright (c) 2005 by the Regents of the University of California. Reprinted with the permission of Alice Notley.

Elizabeth Bishop: "It Is Marvellous . . ." from *Edgar Allan Poe & The Juke-Box: Uncollected Poems, Drafts, and Fragments*. Copyright (c) 2007 by Alice Helen Methfessel. Reprinted by permission of Farrar, Straus and Giroux, LLC.

Star Black: "The Evangelist" copyright (c) 2007 by Star Black. Used with the permission of the poet.

Paul Blackburn: "The Once-Over" from *The Collected Poems of Paul Blackburn*. Copyright (c) 1985 by Paul Blackburn. Reprinted with the permission of Persea Books, Inc.

Robin Blaser: "2nd Tale: Return" from *The Holy Forest*. Copyright (c) 2006 by the Regents of the University of California. Reprinted with the permission of the University of California Press.

Catherine Bowman: "Demographics" from *1–800–HOT-RIBS*. Copyright (c) 1993 by Catherine Bowman. Reprinted with the permission of the author and Gibbs Smith.

Charles Bukowski: "Hunk of Rock" from *The Last Night of the Earth Poems*. Copyright (c) 1992 by Charles Bukowski. Reprinted with the permission of HarperCollins Publishers.

Robert Olen Butler: "Walter Raleigh, courtier and explorer, beheaded by King James I, 1618" from *Severance: Stories*. Copyright (c) 2006 by Robert Olen Butler. Reprinted with the permission of Chronicle Books, San Francisco.

Hayden Carruth: "Assignment" from *Collected Shorter Poems 1946–1991*. Copyright (c) 1991 by Hayden Carruth. Reprinted with the permission of Copper Canyon Press, www.coppercanyonpress.org.

Heather Christle: "Letter to My Love" appeared in *Octopus*. Copyright (c) 2005 by Heather Christle. Reprinted with the permission of the poet.

Lucille Clifton: "to a dark moses" from *Good Woman: Poems and a Memoir 1969–1980*. Copyright (c) 1987 by Lucille Clifton. Reprinted with the permission of BOA Editions, Ltd., www.boaeditions.org.

Marc Cohen: "It Never Happened" copyright (c) 2007 by Marc Cohen. Used with the permission of the poet.

Billy Collins: "Pinup" from *The Art of Drowning*. Copyright (c) 1995 by Billy Collins. Reprinted with the permission of the University of Pittsburgh Press.

Dennis Cooper: "After School, Street Football, Grade Eight" from *The*

INDEX OF POEMS

INDEX OF POETS

A NOTE ON THE TYPE

Stempel Garamond, the typeface used in this book, was created by the Stempel Typefoundry in 1924 for the Linotype Corporation. Stempel Garamond is based upon the type designs of Claude Garamond (1480–1561), the famous French type designer. Stempel Garamond is an old style typeface with a heavy weight, making it highly readable.